Conversations with

Female Millionaires

Discover the Secrets Used by America's Wealthiest Women to Get Rich!

Rachel D. Young & Jason Oman

Visit our website at:
www.ConversationsWithFemaleMillionaires.com

Printed in the United States of America

ISBN 978-0-615-44719-3

ACKNOWLEDGEMENTS:

We'd both like to thank a BUNCH of people for making this book a reality!

Jason would like to thank:

First of all give very special and enormous thanks to his amazing friend and coAuthor Rachel D. Young and all the incredible women in Conversations with Female Millionaires!!

To his mother Merry, (one of the very first people to introduce him to the incredible world of Personal Development), as well as Greg Montoya, John deLisle, Matt Bacak, Devon Brown, Joey Smith, and Gina Gaudio Graves. In addition Jason wants to thank his amazing mastermind partners Ronda Del Boccio (ProfitableStoryTelling.com), Kennon Fort (KillPainFast.com), Michael Savoie, Yvonne Lyon, and JP Maroney.

You've all made more of an amazing positive difference than you may ever know!!

Rachel would like to thank:

To my loving family, whose understanding and patience made a LOT of this book possible!

To the ladies who appear in this book – thank you for your willingness to share and the openness and humility you showed during each of your interviews.

To the readers of this book – thank you for allowing Jason and I into your hearts and minds. It's our hope that you take away something life-changing during this read that you can apply to your entrepreneurial endeavors and become wildly successful as a result!

FOREWORD

Women are different. There's no argument there.

We go to the bathroom in groups.

We notice a new haircut or pair of shoes on our best girlfriend before she's even had a chance to say hello! We can spend hours talking over a single cup of coffee without ever noticing the time – we're so involved in each others' conversation!

Women even run and view business differently!

As of the writing of this book, women account for over half of the businesses started in the United States today.

Women outnumber men in college graduations.

Women are truly making an impact in the global economy.

So why read other "Success" books written *by* men, *for* men, if we're such different creatures when it comes to *creating our own success and wealth*?

In the foreword to Think and Grow Rich by Napoleon Hill, the question was asked, "What do you want most?"

If you're an entrepreneurial woman (or aspire to be one), chances are 'Success' is one of your top 3 answers. The book you're now reading holds many of the keys to that answer of "Success".

Sitting in Donald Trump's boardroom on the first season of The Apprentice, I remember thinking, "I'm in the presence of one of the richest men in the world. I have so many questions I'd like to ask him!"

Mr. Trump was very generous with his knowledge and understanding of the world of business.

Granted, I'd already been successful in my own right, but his was a level of wealth and success that I'd only dreamt of!

But it was him saying, "If you're already going to be thinking, think big" that changed everything!

The women in the book you're about to read know how to "think big". They do it every day.

You're about to learn from millionaire women who have dominated their niches and industries in a male-dominated society!

I got so excited when I was reading Conversations with Female Millionaires!

The successful women featured here don't just talk about success, they obviously LIVE it!

They know what it is to take action, to lead others, to come from nothing, to support other women who also want to be successful.

You're holding in your hands the book that could create such a dramatic change in your life that you accomplish, create, and do more in the next 12 months than you ever have before!

Learning from the success of others is smart.

Learning from the success of other entrepreneurial women who are already doing what you want to do and are willing to share exactly how you can do it as well is genius.

Conversations with Female Millionaires can help you do just that.

So get your highlighter, pen, and paper handy because, if you're like me, you'll want to take lots of notes!

To your lifelong success,
Kristi Frank
CEO, SaturdayMorningSuccess.com
Season 1, The Apprentice

Table of Contents

Chapter 6 - Conversation with Terri Levine
The Coaching Guru
Why Selling Sucks…How to Sell without Manipulation…Finding Your True Gifts…How to Know When You've Found the Right Business to Be In

Chapter 7 - Conversation with Sydney Biddle Barrows
Former Mayflower Madam Turned Experience Coach
Falling into Success…How to Give Good "Wow" in Any Industry…A Case of Dom Can Make You Millions!...Why Any Business (Even Call Girls) Can and Should Have a Guarantee

Chapter 8 - Conversation with Sandra Yancey
CEO, Founder eWomenNetwork
How Setbacks Can Lead to Bigger Success…Five Minutes Before the Miracle Happens…What to Do When You Hit Rock Bottom…Preparing to Be Successful

Chapter 1:

Kim Kiyosaki, Author of Rich Woman

Rachel D. Young: Kim, first of all, thank you so much for being a part of this very powerful book! We want to help eliminate a lot of the excuses that, I think, we as women have when it comes to taking that first step. Then taking the second step, and worrying about fear, and failure, and everything in between.

KK: Yeah, that first step… I mean a lot of what we focus on now is giving the education just to give women the confidence to act.

You know, they can read all they want. They can study all they want. They can go to seminar after seminar. But, until they **go out and *do* something…** Whether it's business, whether it's investing, it's just getting over that first hurdle. Which I find is the most difficult for men *and* women. But, especially for women!

I think a lot of it has to do with the fact that we are brought up and raised to be caretakers, and nurturers, and take care of everyone else.

RDY: Right. Right.

And starting a business seems like kind of a selfish endeavor. I mean, you *are* making the money to give to your family. But, it takes a lot of your time, a lot of your effort, and your focus.

So, you feel sometimes, especially as a mom, I call it mommy guilt. Where you feel like you should be giving to the other members of your family.

KK: Yeah. I see that a lot. We tend to put everybody else first. And we put ourselves last! Even just wanting to come to a woman's seminar. Even that, they feel guilty about. It's like 'I'm taking time for myself!' Well, if you don't take the time for yourself, and you don't build your business, or you don't build your wealth, then you're doing your family a disservice! So, they get that 'mindset shift' takes a lot. It's like women think that they *have* to be there all the time! And that is the best thing…

RDY: Yeah. That's it exactly!

Alright, so, first of all, you're like the *Foremost* expert in the world on 'women' and 'finance'! I *Googled* 'Women's Financial Education' and you were *all* over the front page!

Even the name of your book, *"Rich Woman"*, for heaven's sake. That says it all in my opinion…

But, if I'm remembering correctly from reading all of the *Rich Dad* and *Rich Woman* books over the years, it wasn't always the case. You were not always on top!

I mean, weren't you and Robert homeless for a while?

KK: Yes. Robert and I met in 1984, and we say 1985 was the worst year of our lives! What happened is, at my very first job out of college I was very, very excited! I went to work in an Advertising Agency. My background was marketing and advertising. So, I went to start an Advertising Agency. And after almost a year, I was fired by my boss! She and I just did *not* get along. So, it was kind of devastating!

I was like, 'Oh, my God, I got fired!' So, while I was working at another job, I got a call from that same agency. They had fired her, actually, and they wanted to hire me back! So, they hired me back. And about six months later, they fired me again! So, I was like, *what* is wrong with this?? I'm blaming everybody and it was just going on and on… Finally, I was just like "Ok, what do I need to do?" Because I hate being told what to do.

That really *was* the case! So, I'm like, 'I think I need to start a business.' But, I didn't grow up with anybody who was a business owner. My parents were employees. So, I didn't know where to start. I wasn't hanging out without anybody who was an entrepreneur. On the first date Robert and I had back in '84 he asked me, "What do you want to do with you life?" I said, "Well, seeing as I don't do very well taking orders from other people, I really want my own business." He said, "I can help you with that." We met in February. About a month later I had started my first very small business!

I created that so we could travel. I had that business and I also had a part time job. Then, in December I left that job and left that business behind. He shut down his factory and we set off to California to build our next business. And with everything we had, which wasn't a lot, in about two to three months we were flat broke! It was simply that we thought, you know, *our business would be up and running*. But, it took a whole lot longer and we ran out of money. We were sleeping on people's floors. We slept in an old beat up, brown Toyota Celica. There were weekends where… especially one weekend I remember...

Robert was away teaching for a friend of his for free. I had two dollars to get me through three days. And it was really a very, very, very, very tough time! Because, up until that point, I was always very optimistic. I could be doing anything, and whatever I wanted just seemed to appear! But, now all of a sudden, *nothing* was working!

The hardest thing was the shot that my self-esteem took! It pretty much plummeted into the toilet!

And to pull myself out of that and for both of us to stay together during that time was tough enough. Because there were times we both wanted to quit on the relationship and on the business!

But, we just kept going and didn't quit!

I think one of the things I'm most proud of, one of the *best* accomplishments is that we didn't quit!

You know, people said, "Why don't you just go back, and get a job, and put this business aside?" But, we knew that if we did that, that we would never continue it!

So, we struggled for a good year and a half.

Then, after the business was up and running, we finally did pay ourselves! I remember it was about a year later, and our first check that we paid ourselves was $1,500 and we were ecstatic!

So, we worked really hard for a year for $1,500! Then just little by little we grew it.

But, that time of being homeless and broke, was a very, very difficult time! In retrospect, it was probably one of the best things that could have happened to us! Because it really built our character and helped make us who we are today!

So, the adversity actually…I have learned this over the years, adversity can be one of the greatest gifts of all!

RDY: Did you already have an awareness of the need for your own financial education at this point?

KK: I didn't know anything about money or finances. It was not even a thought!

I was always very independent. Even as a kid…I'm the youngest of three girls.

I remember when I was in High School we took a trip.

I was the only daughter that ever had a job in High School. And we took this family trip to Hawaii. The deal was we had to pay for our own airfares.

And, being the youngest, I was the only one of the three that paid.

In college my parents would send me a little bit of money to survive on every month. And I remember the first year of college I called them and said, "Don't send me any more money. I have a job. I'm fine."

So, I never wanted to be dependent on people for money. But, I didn't understand anything about investing! I didn't understand about growing your money.

I was brought up… You know, you get a job, and you work your way up, and you get a pay raise. That's what I was told. So, I didn't have any education or any knowledge in that field at all.

RDY: Now, that's kind of interesting! Because, in my experience, a lot of women view "Financial Education" as the equivalent of being back in Algebra class in High School.

You know, 'If your money is getting on a train and leaving Chicago at 3:30 in the afternoon going 100 miles an hour' type thing…But, it's not like that!

I think it's scarier to be uninformed than it is to take the steps to learn!

KK: Oh, absolutely! I mean, here's what I find with women, Rachel…

Number one, I think most of us have been taught…If you look how young girls are brought up, it's still the Prince Charming story.

It's still the traditional roles. I mean, I always fought against the *Traditional Female Role* all my life! I was into sports. I was independent. I didn't *ever* want to get married! It was like I fought it!

But, most women, at least when I was growing up and I still think it happens today…We're taught to actually be dependent on somebody for our financial well being.

Not only do most of us not have the Financial Education…
But, from an early age, we're kind of taught that your
husband will provide for you. Your family will provide for
you.

There's very little talk about the 'financial role' for women.

Then, I think what happens for so many women is that they
don't make their financial life a priority until they have a
wakeup call.

So, today especially, with all the job lay-offs happening…It
could be a divorce. It could be the death of a spouse, or a
family member, where all of the sudden the woman is
either left to fend for herself, or she loses her source of
income!

It's like, "Oh, my! Now what do I do?" And, it's not until
this wakeup call happens where the woman goes, 'Oh, my!
I had better to do something about my financial life!'

My whole premise is, *why not prepare now?* Hopefully you
will never have that wake-up call…But, you can prepare
now!

There are things you can do now, so if anything were to
happen, you'll be prepared for whatever comes your way!

RDY: You know, I was flipping through the channels the
other night on TV and I came across some special about
Child Beauty Pageants. The mom was grooming her three
daughters for their next pageant.

She was very proud of them and said, "I have always taught
them to be self-sufficient. So, they can go out and do their

own thing. But, they also use the tools that they learn in these Beauty Pageants in case they want to marry an ambassador when they grow up?"

I'm serious!...I was kind of like... ***why can't they be the ambassador?***

KK: Yeah, exactly! Oh, so true.

I have a niece and she's very artistic and doesn't have a lot of financial sense even though I send her all the books…

She's just a very, very free spirit! She was dating this young man from a well-to-do family. And my sister said to me, "Well, maybe she will just marry him and that will be the best thing!"

So, I looked at her and I said, "Do you know what I *do*? Do you know *what* I teach? That's the *last* thing you should be thinking!..." *(Laughter)*

And *so* many people think *that* is security!...

They're finding out today, whether it's divorce, or job layoffs, it's *not* security!

But, the more important thing is, why are women not taught early on to take care of yourself financially?

RDY: Yes! I remember when I first got to college...I grew up in Japan. My parents were missionaries, and money was *never* talked about at all in our house! Never, ever, ever!

They dropped me off at college here in the states with a credit card, a checking account, a new car, and they went back to Japan.

I remember going shopping with my girlfriends the very first time. I said, "You guys, I don't have any money." And they said, "Well, don't you have a checkbook?"

And I said, "Well, yeah."

And they said, "Well, just write a check!"

I remember standing at the counter at Sears, and the lady behind the counter was showing me how to fill out a check. I had no clue!

I was like, "Ok, so what goes here?... Oh, Sears. Ok, I'll write that. Oh, why do I have to write the amount twice? You know, once in long hand and once with numbers?..."

I mean, she looked at me like, *'What? Have you been living under a rock for your entire life? Why do you not know this?'*

And I thought as long as I had checks I could keep going!...

KK: Oh, that's funny! I can tell you a story of a woman, 57 years old, and not too long ago her husband unexpectedly passed away. She didn't know how to write a check!

I mean, she was just oblivious! He handled everything! And I think, too, that it's *such* a disservice for the spouse to think that they're really taking care of their wife. But, they're really putting her in a great danger!

I see more and more when the husband does pass away, then all these helpers: Mr. and Mrs. Financial Planner come and say, "Oh, let me take care of your money."

And they take care of it straight into their own pockets!

RDY: Well, now let me ask you this, because you were echoing what I said, 'money was never talked about in our household' and I kind of heard you agreeing a little bit…

I think a lot of women, and a lot of times people in general, have this image of *money is the root of all evil...*

Or, it's 'hard earned money', or it's 'cold hard cash', 'fat cat bankers', you know, whatever.

Do you think that the amount of money that a woman has, let's say she has been in business for a while, the amount of money that a woman has is in direct proportion to her view of it? I mean, can a woman hate the thought of being successful, or rich, and still have money?

KK: I don't think so. I mean she could *have* money like she could inherit it or something.

But, she will probably lose it very quickly! I'm a believer in 'You ultimately get what you want.' And you *are* your thoughts!

So, if you think money is evil, then it will be.

And if you think that, you know, the rich are greedy. This is when... when I was flat broke before this all happened, *I* thought that the rich were mean and greedy!

Well, I will tell you, when I was flat broke, *I* was pretty mean and *I* was pretty greedy! And the stress and the arguments between me and Robert, it was terrible.

It's a horrible place to be.

So, if you have the thought that 'Money is bad', then you are not going to want to have money around you!

Now, this is how I look at it…If you *are* making money successfully, all you are doing is delivering what is needed and wanted!

If today a person is out of work, and they are not making money, and they can't find a job, it's because what they are offering is not needed and wanted in the market place. I mean, I see it that simple!

I look at the job of an entrepreneur is very simply to solve problems!

You know, they see a big problem that needs to be solved and they go tackle it!

Steve Jobs wanted computers in every home. He saw that as the problem and he went after it!

Richard Branson took on British Air, and the big record companies.

Most entrepreneurs go into business because they see a problem and they want to solve it.

As an entrepreneur, or even just as an employee, if your goal is simply to make money, you are *not* going to do very well! Because you have got to have a greater purpose for your being on this planet, I believe.

Robert and I, we might have a money goal. But, our goal, our purpose, our mission has nothing to do with money!

We just know that if we keep doing what we are supposed to be doing, and if we have a big enough mission, and if people want what we are producing, then money will come in! It is kind of a score card for us. If we're doing what we're supposed to be doing then the money will come!

And it's not 'do what you love and the money will follow'. You *can* do what you love, but you have got to work your butt off! And then the money will maybe follow.

KK: But, if somebody has an issue with money and thinks that money is bad, I would literally go see somebody about that!

I have a coach that handles all of my crazy thoughts for personal development. I will sit down and we'll do some processes. I'm like, "I have got this funny thought". Or, sometimes I don't even know what the thought is that I was having.

But, if you think money is bad, and if you hate being rich and successful, I don't think you can be. I don't think you can be.

But, if the goal is to be rich and successful, you're probably never going to get there anyway. Because there is going to be a 'means'. It is *how* you earn your money that really determines your wealth! Make sense?

RDY: Oh, absolutely, absolutely! I think a lot of women don't take the time to understand the concept of money. That it's more than just the paper it is printed on. It is your idea of it…

You are seeing a lot of women now, especially from the Baby Boomer Generation that were raised by Depression era parents.

I mean, my Great Grandmother, when she passed away…We used to wonder why sleeping on her sofas was so uncomfortable when we would go and visit her. It was because they were stuffed full of money!

KK: I love it.

RDY: Literally, $50,000 in a sofa! She had just crammed money into it rather than putting it in a bank.

So, I think a lot of women don't understand that whole concept of making money work for you, or learning what an actual 'P&L Sheet' is, and how to fill one out. And it's kind of scary at first…

KK: Yeah, well, you mean the whole subject of Financial Education?

Yeah. It is. It can be very overwhelming. It can be very intimidating.

I tell them, the first thing you do is just get a Financial Dictionary. Because often times... I know you've seen it on the financial TV shows: CNBC, or MSNBC, these experts with all this jargon: The Derivative, The PE Ratio, and The Cap Rate.

I sort of got that they do it to make themselves look and sound smart. Because, I have questioned when I have been looking at property with Real Estate Agents, and they will use all this jargon, and I will ask them… 'Can you explain what a Cap Rate is exactly?'

'Oh, well it's ... it's an indicator.'

I said, "Of what?"

You know, I've questioned them, and they don't even know what it is!

So, I don't know why people want to make it so complicated. Because it's not. And what people find out through education is that it's not Rocket Science.

I mean, to me the purpose of financial education, for women, is simply freedom. Freedom from, you know, money can either enslave a woman by being in a marriage that is terrible, or being in a job that she hates.

People can use that as control, or the other side of it, is money can free you!

So, learning how to make your money grow...

I don't mind talking about how to manage your money. You know, putting it in a 401k which actually is probably the worst investment you could ever get into! But, that's another subject.

They tell you the simple... you know, like 401k, and a CD, and save money. Which is more bad advice given in today's economic terms.

And, they tell you all these things to do that you're never going to get wealthy by doing... The 'Managing your money', etc.

You really have to take some time, study, put some money down, and learn how to make your money work *for* you!

You know, if you have $1000, how can that $1000 make you $100 or $200 dollars a year?

If women could learn that, because they are very, very good at it. I think they are very, very good at it…

RDY: Now, it seems like when you start getting into the whole idea of 'Financial Education', then the more you read, the more you learn, the more you realize that there is a lot that you don't know that you don't know!

Is that lack of knowledge and education about money in general, is that generational and a familial issue? Or, are we, as women, just not properly educating ourselves? I mean, where does that lack of education come from?

KK: Well, number one, just as you have said, Rachel, it is very, very, very *few* women I have talked to whose families ever discuss money!

I mean, to this day, my father will *not* talk about money to me!

You know, I have to go around his back and ask mom, "How are you guy's doing? How are you doing? What is happening?" Because, he doesn't want to talk about it.

So, I think #1: it comes from parents.

#2: it comes from our school system. It does not talk about money.

Some *are* starting to talk about it now. But, their idea of Financial Education is bringing in a local Stock Broker, or the local Banker who is looking for future clients.

You know, there is not really anybody in the school system that I have seen, except for a few rare cases, where they're actually bringing legitimate Financial Education to the students. So, one of the biggest things that I see the school system do, and this could be a book in itself... I have seen young kids go into school, I was one of them. I was so excited and I was really pumped up!... *'Alright, I'm going to school, and I'm going to do all this stuff!'*

I was so excited! And then you just get punished up one side and down another...

You made this mistake. You spelled this word wrong. You got an F because you couldn't add. And it was just so much...They just basically annihilate you!

So, kids come out of school terrified of making a mistake...But, the only way to succeed in business, or succeed in investing, is to make a lot of mistakes!

Because that is how we learn. So, actually when we created the *CashFlow* board game, which was our very first product before *Rich Dad, Poor Dad*, we had this great idea...

We figured the women would move this game, because it would teach financial education, and we would take it to the universities. What a great idea!

So, we took it to Harvard. We had a contact there. We sent them the game and asked them, 'Would a group of women get together to play the game?'

I called them to follow up, and this woman says, "Well, this is Harvard. We don't teach money at Harvard. And I'm like, "Oh, ok."

They said, "By the way, women don't play games!"

And I went... "What planet are *you* on?" Women are the best game players on the planet! But, there is like a stigma that is like 'Money is beneath us.' You know, Academia is above money. So, I think that is another place.

Then, the third, is just the Societal Stigma that gets put on women. That the husband is supposed to provide. I think finally that is all coming crashing down now given this economy, and I think the economy has changed forever.

Here's what I am excited about in this financial crisis, is that often times, women don't really step up to the forefront unless they are put in an emergency. Unless there is some kind of crisis.

So, I have seen, in many families, when there is a financial crisis, it is the <u>woman</u> that steps up and says, "*I* will take care of things. I will handle it. I will figure it out!"

And so, I see this time right now in history, as being a time where I think we are going to have a lot of women stepping up into business and stepping up into the financial world. Because they can't sit back and hide, if that is what they were doing. But, they are going to be forced into forefront which I think is very exciting!

RDY: That *is* exciting! I hadn't even look at it that way. But, yeah, even in my own family, I did the exact same thing as far as stepping up to the plate and being the one who says, "No, I will get it done."

But, as far as the schooling goes, you are preaching to the choir on this one. Because, my husband and I homeschool our children for that very reason! So, I'm curious, though, at least on the East Coast, where I do a lot of my speaking, a lot of women claim to be bad at Math. Especially in the south where I'm from you hear that all the time.

Especially from my own mother! When we first played your *CashFlow* game, my mother was kicking and screaming! There were fingernail marks in the floor dragging her to the kitchen table… 'I'm not good at math. I'm going to be terrible at this game.'

She won.

KK: Oh, see? There you go.

RDY: But, a lot of women seem to be in charge of the finances, and these are the same women that are saying that they're bad at math.

KK: Yeah, I don't know where that comes from, because I hear the same thing from women. I hear things like, *'My eyes glaze over when I look at the numbers.'*

Or *'My husband wants me to go to our meeting with our Financial Planner, but I just can't think that way.'* And they're kind of proud of it! I don't understand that.

But, it's like a skill that women think they aren't supposed to have. But, as I said earlier, it is not Rocket Science!

And when women *do* step in and take charge, I mean, once they learn it and once they get involved in it, and study, and learn, they are brilliant at it!

As you said earlier, Rachel, women are nurturers. Well, we also nurture our portfolios! You know, I nurture my properties! I want the tenants to have a nice place to live, and want to recommend it to their friends! I want to nurture the property, and make sure it is better every year, and not deteriorating.

So, those same skills that women are very good at, translate very, very well into the world of money!

I was talking at an event on Friday in LA…We were talking about the Stock Market crash. And I said, "When the Stock Market crashes, it's a *Sale!* It's like a Sale at Macy's! You should be running in there and buying as much as you can."

And that is the attitude. We *know* how to spot a bargain! Once we *know* what to look for, and what the criteria is, we can spot a bargain!

So, I think a lot of the *Natural Instincts* many women have translate very, very well in the world of money!

And when you talk about the fact that women control the... I think the statistic is like 80% of the family finances are controlled by women. Well, really what they are controlling is they are paying the bills, and they are more focused on the household goals. Like, the furnishings and things for the house. But, in 90% of the cases, that does *not* apply to investing!

When you look at who is making the investment decisions, it is usually the husband. Unless there's not a husband in the house and she has to make the decisions. But, then the question is: Is she doing what she needs to do to become financially secure?

RDY: Do you know what I think? When I first started thinking about the idea of investing…I used to work for a phone company. That was one of the things they offered, was that you could have a certain amount of your paycheck go towards buying company stock.

I thought of it that way. Or, I thought I had to have been in business for a while and be a huge conglomerate that would then be able to go out and invest.

Because I assumed that you either needed to have a lot of money, or you had to somehow be a part of the corporation in order to invest. Can you just talk a little bit more about that? Because I know I'm not alone in that thinking.

KK: Yes. It's because of the financial magazines, newspapers, and the TV shows. They make it sound so complicated. They use all this jargon.

But, if you just look up some of the words, you can find out that it's not that complicated. I think women need to find, and this is the key, is who do you take your advice from? And, who do you get your financial information from?

I think *that* is really a key! Because, there's so much information out there! How do you sift through it all to find the information you need?

So, I would say this for women… The first step, the first question I ask women, and it usually makes people very uncomfortable is, *"If you stopped working today, or you and your husband stopped working today, so no more paycheck, no more salary… How long could you survive given the same standard of living you have today?"*

So, if you don't have the paycheck, you don't have the salary, how much do you have in savings and CDs?

Maybe you have some Cash Flow Investments. How long will that money last given your current standard of living? So, for some people, it might be 10 years. For a lot of people, it's less than three months! For a *lot* of people, it is less than a month!

So, a lot of people are just barely living paycheck to paycheck! But, it doesn't really matter what that number is.

It's just that that is where you are. So, if that's where you are financially, if that's the case, do you want to be dependent on your paycheck, and on your job, and even on your business given this economy?

If not, then start looking for 'financial education'…There are four primary Asset Classes: Business, Real Estate, Paper Assets (like Mutual Funds & Commodities), and Precious Metals (like Gold & Silver).

And you start to see which one is of most interest, which one do I really want to learn about. You just start studying that, and finding where the good information is, and what resonates with you.

Then, once you have a little bit of financial education, then the most important thing is you have got to put a little bit of money down to get started.

Don't bet the ranch. Don't spend your mortgage payment, just a little bit of money. Because when you put a little bit of money down, then your interest level skyrockets!

RDY: Well, let me ask you this, because I had a workshop recently where I gave out copies of *Rich Woman*...

I offered them in drawings. And there was one lady in particular that of all the Door Prizes that I had, that was the one that she zeroed in on! She said, "I want this book so badly!" So, I met with her later after the event.

She said, "You know, I've been reading this book. I'm so excited! But, I've never invested in anything before. I do nails for a living. I barely have enough to cover my own bills. How in the world can I invest in anything?"

KK: I hear it all the time. I hear it all the time. I can just answer it this way...

I did a little bit of investing in Gold and Silver before '89. But, we're talking about Real Estate. So, in '89 Robert said "It's time you started investing."

I'm like, "What? Are you kidding me? Only the really wealthy and successful people invest in Real Estate!"

He starts laughing and started to explain what his *Rich Dad* taught him about Real Estate Investing. He says, "Ok, go, go try it." But, at that time, I had no money. We had no money.

This was just after the $1,500 that we paid ourselves.

So, I had little to no money. There are two things that we did, and I talked about it in the book.

You know, the 3 Piggy Banks...

Pay yourself first: With every dollar that came into our household, we took a percentage off the top. For us, it was 30%. Because, that was a big stretch for us!

We put 10% into a savings account, and 10% into an investment account, and 10% into a 'Charity or Tithing' account.

The trick was that that came off the top, before we paid any bills!

Then you had to get really, really creative on how you were going to pay your bills, because we weren't going to walk out on our bills!

We wanted to make sure that everybody that we borrowed from or everybody we owed money to was paid!

But, that habit alone, of paying ourselves first, off the top, was the main thing that allowed us to invest, number one.

Then, the second thing is, when I did find that first property, this little 2-bedroom, 1-bath house in Portland, Oregon, I needed $5,000 as a down payment. And, I will tell you... When you don't have the money, and you see a deal, and you think that this could be it, you do whatever you can to come up with that down payment!

So, we got really creative. We actually created very, very quickly a new product that we could sell to our database. That was one thing we did. Then, we figured out where to get some other funds.

Long story short, it was called an Assumable Loan. So, the loan was attached to the house.

So, again, the whole thing about people's excuses of not having money, I don't buy it. Because, we hear all the time, "When I have the money, I will invest."

KK: But, they never have the money. You never have the money! So, I always say, *"Find the investment first and get excited about it! Then, put your brain to work on how you are going to come up with the money."*

It might be borrowing it from family or friends. That's a little dicey. So, you need a really tight iron-clad *agreement*. But, there's all sorts of ways to find the money once you find the investment.

But, if you're going to wait until you have the money, there is always something that is going to eat up the money! You know, the new tires, or you want to go out to the movies, or whatever it is. So, the excuses I hear are, *'I don't have enough money. I'm not smart enough. And I don't have enough time.'* But, in my world those are just excuses. They are just reasons, just women saying, "I don't want to do this."

RDY: Wow. So, let me ask you this…If there are 3 Piggy Banks, if the deal is good enough, and you were back in that same situation with that very first house in Portland, and you had between the 3 Piggy Banks you had $5,000, would you have taken it from there?

KK: Yeah. Except that, well let me back up. The tithing we still do. The Savings Account and Investment Account have been blended into one.

So, we only save in...And, you know, another one of the rules that have changed is that people used to be able to retire on their Savings. Because, they would have Savings with a nice Interest Rate, or they would have a Pension from their job.

They would have what is called the *Defined Benefits Plan* where the company is basically, like a Pension Plan. So, you could retire from your Savings.

But, you cannot today retire off your Savings at 0% - 1% Interest with a 401k that is tied to the Stock Market where more people have lost 20 – 50% of their 401Ks.

So that thinking doesn't apply anymore. That rule has changed. So, we don't save Long Term. We only save Short Term until a good investment comes along.

Then, we would rather put our money into a Real Estate deal, or into Gold and Silver, or into an oil deal. Because we're going to get a better return on our money than just letting it sit in the bank and get eaten away.

And with all the money that they're printing today, of course, your money is worth less and less.

RDY: Right. So, if I'm hearing right, I heard you talk about workshops, and speaking, and you have the book. You have a lot on your plate. But, I know that you and I both are kind of 'Serial Entrepreneurs'. So, we can't stop.

So, I bet you've got something else that you are working on now, am I right?

KK: Here's the main thing I'm working on, Rachel... This is interesting, because I was at this seminar called

BraveHeart Women. Great organization, a woman named Ellie Drake runs it and she just does a great job with it.

There were a few women entrepreneurs there, and we were talking, and I really got very clear of the main thing I want to do right now.

Because a lot of the women in the audience, you know, they want to get started. But, they don't know *how* to get started.

They are reading the books and they are attending the seminars…

So, right now, what I want to do is, what we're working on is, how to use the technology that is available today, and changing every single minute, you know, with the social media, with the web, with the… even the web is disappearing, the internet and all the apps taking over. And how to use that technology to get the information to as many people as possible throughout the world.

So, we are experimenting with all sorts of… I do have a new Rich Woman book coming out in 2011.

I don't have a title for it yet. Right now it's called *Rich Woman II*. But, that is not the title.

It will be following the women in the *Rich Woman* book, what their particular journeys were, and all the paths they took, and mistakes they made, and choices they made, and choices they didn't make.

That will be a new book following the women in the *Rich Woman* book. About what their particular journeys were, and all the paths they took, and mistakes they made, and choices they made, and choices they didn't make. That will be a new book.

Then, later this year, on RichWoman.com, we are coming out with the *Rich Woman Journey* which is basically a step by step follow the dots.

You know, you're going down this road, read this, study this, watch this. Now, 'I'm interested in real estate.' *If you're interested in real estate follow this path and here is steps to take. If you are interested in stock options, here are the steps to take.*

So, really what I have come down to is that at *Rich Woman* and *Rich Dad*, we don't like to tell people what to do, we just like to say, this is what we have done. And now you need to make your choice.

And what I am seeing is, people want to be told what to do. They really do and especially in this time.

So, you know, I'm stepping up and saying, "Do this. Do this. Do this. Do this."

Then, they'll have decisions to make all along the way of which they want to go. But, at some point, we wanted to give them a pretty robust path to follow. So, we can somewhat hold their hand.

Some pretty important things are coming out as we're putting all these other stories from other women together who, just like you and me, have just started, and they've had their successes...
We're learning things like...

What did they learn?
What mistakes did they make?
And that is becoming a great learning forum for women because they're learning from other women.

RDY: Wow! So, now I have one final question and this one is kind of selfish because it's for me.All the other questions were for the readers...This one is for me.

If you had to do it all over again, and there's a reason that I'm asking, and you had to do it without the support of Robert, would you be where you are now?

KK: Do I think I would be where I am now? No. And I would say only because he and I are so...We basically are together 24/7, and we have done so much!

We have been in partnership since two months after we met. So, I wouldn't be where I am today. I would be in a different place.

But, I don't know what that different place is. I don't know what other choices I would have made. So, I could be really in a terrible place, in a very destitute place.

I could be doing similar to what I'm doing now. I'm pretty much guaranteed this... I do not think I would be teaching women about money and investing. Because that was not even in my radar screen!

But, what I would be doing, and what kind of situation I would be in, I have no idea. Because, I don't know what choices I would have made. I know I would have still been independent. I know I may be not be married. But, it's interesting. Because, when I met Robert, I was actually moving to New York City.

I was born in Honolulu, and I loved advertising. So, I was going to go to Madison Avenue, get a job on Madison Avenue, and work my way up the corporate ladder. Which would have been a huge mistake, because I already knew that was not the path for me.

And one of the things I realized now, looking back, when I was fired twice from that first job is the reason I was fired was because I was so excited about learning business.

So, I went into the job and my boss Dorene wanted me, you know, right by her side. She was the media director and I was her assistant.

So, I would finish what she would want. Then I would go help the Account Executive. And I would help the Production Department. And I would help the Art Department. What I realized is that I didn't want to learn a job… I really wanted to learn the business!
That is what I was excited about!

And so that is where we kept hitting heads. But, I can't answer if I would be better off, or worse off, or the same. I know I would probably be doing something different.

RDY: All right, well, I asked because I started my first business while I was living in my car. And, without the support of my husband being 100 percent behind everything that we have done.

I am quite certain I would *not* be where I am now!

I probably would have gone back and done the 9-to-5 thing and not been pleased with it. But, I think that is the direction my life would have taken.

And I've always wondered of the ladies who were successful, and who had a support system in place, if that was an important piece?

KK: You know, that *so* important! That support system is so crucial! And, if it's not your spouse...

There's a lot of women I have worked with who are single. And, it's like, somewhere you have got to find a support first. Whether it's one individual or whether it's a group.

In the entrepreneur world there is an organization called "EO", Entrepreneur Organization. It used to be YEO, which is a group of entrepreneurs. It's a very good organization. They really hold each other accountable, and they brainstorm, and its like-minded people who all want to support one another growing their business.

I think that is one of the keys to success, is having a support like that. Have people around you. Surround yourself with people who are going to support your vision. I am very, *very* careful who I tell my goals to!
Because I don't want to tell them to somebody who's going to say, "Oh, you can't do that. That's ridiculous. You will never succeed."

So, over the years, I've made a very *conscious* effort to get those negative people out of my life! I have to surround myself with people who are encouraging me, who are pushing me to go beyond where I think I can go. And I think *that* is the key to success!

People who, in many cases, that was Robert for me... I would get comfortable and he would go, "Ok, what is the next step?" So, whether you are single, or married, I think having supportive people around you is crucial for success! I don't know if it's possible without that!

Whether that's a mentor, or a coach, or friends, or people in your industry. I think that is a key. And I didn't know that early on either.

Our formula has always been: We build our business, and we focus on building that business. And it's the Cash Flow from our business that buys our investments.

And then the Cash Flow from our investments buys all of our toys and luxuries! So, that has always been our formula.

RDY: That is... I mean, it makes so much sense though, to build your business up first and since you have that extra. Instead you spread yourself so thin!

KK: Right! And if you're building a business, as you know, it takes everything you've got!

And so you don't want to be, you know, doing a Real Estate deal for the first time and also trying to build a business. Just focus on building that business. Get that stable. Get that cash flowing. And then do the next thing. That is what I found.

RDY: I have just appreciated this interview so very much!

KK: Oh, it has been fun. It has been really fun!

RDY: It really has! Thank you so very much for taking the time to talk with me!

KK: You're very welcome, Rachel.

Jason Oman's comment on Kim Kiyosaki chapter

Near the beginning of this chapter Kim said, "If you *are* making money successfully, all you are doing is delivering what is needed and wanted!"

This really simplifies the entire process of entrepreneurial success! So, make sure to focus on how you can do this too!

Also, take time to study and prepare for your financial future. Learn how to make money work *for* you! Start studying more about doing this. This book reveals where some of the good information is. So check it out and see what resonates with you. IE: Sit down every day with a book on financial education.

Once you have some solid financial education, the next step is to put a little bit of money down to get started.

So, find an investment and get excited about it! Then, put your mind to work on how you can come up with the money to make that small investment to start with.

It's that simple: Take action to get educated. Then take action to find the money to invest. Then take action to invest it. And be persistent - never quit!

Chapter 2:

Lee Milteer – Author, Speaker, Coach

Rachel D. Young: Lee, first of all, I want to say thank you for taking the time to share with us the information, the success, the prestige, everything that comes with it that you have been able to obtain in your life! I just wanted to thank you right up front for taking the time with us today.

Lee Milteer: Thank you. I'm grateful for somebody noticing.

RDY: Now, I wanted to get right off the bat... I know that from hearing you speak several times that you were raised on a farm.

LM: Correct.

RDY: And from personal experience, farm life is hard. ou don't get Christmas and Thanksgiving off. Your birthdays are often spent watering something, counting heads of something, or picking something.

How did that kind of upbringing, that you went through, influence your life as a Business Woman and as an Entrepreneur?

LM: Rachel, it was one of the most important things of my life to learn this incredible work ethic.

I did grow up on a farm. It was a farm slash ranch. We had 110 acres of actual farm where we had herds of cattle. We had horses. We had peacocks. We had dogs. We had cats. We had, you know, goats. We had everything. And, you know, anything that needs to be fed has to be taken care of.

So, my job was to get up at 4:45 every single morning of my life and my job was the horses. I took care of all the horses morning and noon and what it did for me...

By the way, I did not appreciate this as a child at all. You know, because none of my friends had any of this work ethic. They didn't have to do this kind of stuff. They had tiny little chores, like take out the garbage. And I had huge chores!

So, what happened to me was, I developed very early this responsibility, this understanding of: if you don't do it, it doesn't get done, that you cannot do things halfway.

There are consequences for every action that you have. And, dealing with animals, and dealing with the farm, there are no days off. As you said earlier, Christmas, Thanksgiving, birthdays, everything needs to be fed, everything needs to be watered. You know, plants need to be taken care of.

And so, this experience that I had of growing up was about nature, because I was very isolated from pretty much the rest of the world.
I mean, I lived a mile and a half from the closest paved secondary road on a dirt lane. And I was very isolated from a lot of other people, and a lot of things, and it developed

my intuition, and my ability to listen to my instincts greatly.

I learned to pay attention to life's energy. I could intuit things.

Because, when I was brought up, we were only allowed one hour of television a day. And my father was very, very strong about how nature was your greatest teacher, and that you should be outside as much as possible.

You should be doing things. I hardly ever remember sitting down very much as a child. But, reading was very valued in my family. My father particularly.

I mean, I started reading the newspaper at seven years old, and at the end of the day, we would sit at the table and my father would actually teach me adult lessons by saying, "Ok, we have this challenge, or we have this problem, or we have this situation. What do you think are some of the solutions?"

Now, an average, 7, 9, or 10 year old kid doesn't get that education very often today. So, I was very blessed with an extremely hard childhood where I worked very hard. But, today, Rachel, all of that was like Boot Camp into the real world. Because I have always been self-employed.

The only real job I have ever had was when I was a Rock & Roll disc jockey when I was like 17 years old.

I was 17 years old. But, I told them I was 19. I was still in high school. But, they didn't need to know that as far as I was concerned.

I got this job. Then I went into sales. So, all of that perseverance, all of that work ethic, all of that innovation, all of that creativity, all of that problem solving, and coming up with solutions was like training camp that I got growing up on a farm. It all SO paid off!

The other thing is, when I went into sales, my father said 'No' to everything. You know, "Can I do this? Can I do that?"

"No, no, no." So, "No" meant nothing to me. It just meant a way for me to find a solution to figure out how I could get to do what I wanted to do. And so that made me the perfect sales person. No matter what you said to me, I had another solution. So growing up on a farm was a wonderful thing!

I do want to share a little anecdote with you though...

I just spoke recently to a very large International Company, and it was American Greeting Cards, as a matter of fact. And the gentleman who hired me as a speaker said to me, "You know, you have this great reputation and I had heard about you for a long time. But, there were a lot of great speakers with a lot of great reputations.

But let me tell you why I really hired you...

When I found out that you grew up on a farm, I knew that you had impeccable work ethic. And that is what we wanted for our people. And so that is why we hired you."

I would also like to share with you that, growing up on a farm led me to some lessons that I would hope that parents would pay attention to...

I don't know if you remember. But, I have told this story on stage.

That when I was 12 years old, my father came home one day, and we operated five big farms. We had all these foremen and our main foreman got hurt and was put in the hospital.

My father came home, and I remember this clearly like it was yesterday.

He was sitting in the living room and my father was this six foot five, 250 pound huge guy.

And he looked like he was going to cry. And I walked in and he said to me, "You know, our foreman has been hurt and we have a whole 37 people up in a field that I have no foreman for and they are just sitting there and I don't know what to do."

And, then he looked up to me, and I had a younger brother who was like nine years old at the time, and he said, "Your brother is too little. You are the only one left. Go down to the barn, saddle your horse. Load your rifle. Get your butt up to that field and I want you to take charge of those 37 people."

And that is the day I really became a woman. Because I saddled up, I put the rifle in.

I am, by the way, a sharp shooter. Because when you grow up on a farm, it's something to do.

I don't kill things, by the way. But, I went up to the farm and led these people.

We had crops of peanuts. Acres and acres and acres of peanuts. And when you have people who are low income, and this is their job, all they really want to do is sit down. So, my job was to get them across these long fields of labor and figure out how to be a leader.

I did that when I was 12 years old. I learned to work harder than them, get ahead of them, to push them, to motivate them, to make them appreciate what they were doing.

My nickname at the time was '1 more row'. Because, at the end of each row they wanted to sit down. So, I would always say, "One more row. We can do one more row!"

Within two weeks my father actually hired me full time and put me in charge of the whole crew.

So, at 12 years old, I actually had 37 people working for me and literally was better than all of the other foremen we had. Because I could motivate that crew just by my sheer enthusiasm of how we could do this.

So, it showed me some leadership skills that I had that have led me to where I am today.

So, no matter how daunting the task, there is a solution.

RDY: That is one of my all time favorite stories that you tell. I am so glad that you told it.

LM: Well, actually my husband brought this to my attention a few years ago. He said, "Why don't you tell that story about how you were 12 years old and you had 37 people working for you." And I had actually forgotten it, because there is so many stories like that.

I mean, most of us in life who really strive to be successful, there is a reason you strive to be successful.

The most successful people on earth are extremely insecure. And the reason you are insecure is because you are always being presented with challenges and situations where you have to step up to the ante. You have to perform.

And, you may not be perfect at it. But, it's the difference between average people and really motivated people. Motivated people will take the risk. They don't have to do it perfectly when they first go out. But, they have to believe in their own inner ability to figure out whatever it is they need to do.

My childhood on a farm where there was a lot of tragedy. There was a lot of animals getting killed, or bad things that happened. You just grow up at a faster rate.

I always say to parents, "Any time that you can get your children to take responsibility and be responsible for something, whether it is taking care of pets or taking care of the yard, where that they can see an accomplishment, this is great gifts for them."

And, if I may stand on my soap box for a moment, and say that I am very disturbed today by the attitude that everything is given to children. Because I think it cripples them.

You do not get the knowledge and wisdom that you can have in life if everybody gives you everything.

Plus, it makes you feel entitled. And that's something that if you want to be a millionaire, if you want to be wealthy, if you want to be successful, you always have to understand the responsibility is yours.

It's 100 percent yours. It's not anybody else, and frankly, nobody is going to give you much in life that you don't earn.

RDY: Well, that's why my husband and I homeschool our three kids is so that they can see what a successful business looks like.

That sometimes they get up in the middle of the night and, oh, mom may be at the computer trying to beat a deadline. We just wanted them to see and have that full experience as well.

LM: Absolutely.

RDY: It's funny that you brought up 'success'. Because you grew up on a farm, and I did as well.

You know, a lot of times when there may have been a drought, or if some of the cattle got out, or if there was a plague or pestilence… Point being, there are some things that can influence, or hinder, how well your family eats at any given time.

So, would you say that your surroundings growing up on that farm, did they advance or hinder your idea of what 'Success' was and what you wanted to achieve in life?

LM: I have to tell you, Rachel, as a child, I wasn't surrounded by prosperous people.

This is a very interesting question to me. Because, I hadn't actually thought of this before now.

But, you're right. The homes around us were not exactly prosperous. We were very, very land rich. But, very, very money poor.

My parents were both children of other farmers from as far back as we could trace on both sides. So, the challenge I think I faced as a child is that my parents had no ambition for me as a girl.

Also, my family had this perception that boys were more valuable than girls. Especially on a farm.
I was the first born. So, they were deeply disappointed that I was a girl. They just did not have a value system for females.

So, no one ever said to me as a child anything remotely motivational about success. Except my father did say this to me…

On a repeated basis he would turn to me and say, "I really care what you decide to do in life. However, whatever you decide to do, please do not do anything that average people do."

He said, "I don't know what you're going to do. But, don't do what average people do. Do something in your life that other people aren't doing."

As I got to be about 15 years old, my father did turn to me one day and said, "Look, I think you really need to find something extraordinary to do in life. Because, you are terrible wife material."

By the time I was 16, he was on a real roll about, "You're not wife material at all. You have got to find yourself a great career."

And all of that was very true.

Because, I was a very independent and head strong.

I would get on my horse in the morning. I would ride 25 miles away. Nobody would see me until almost night fall.

There were no cell phones. So, it's like, 'I guess she is ok.'

I lived my whole 11th and 12th year in high school in the guidance counselor's office. Pretty much desperate to figure out what on earth I was going to do with my life. Because I didn't fit into any category that was a typical 'Female Category'.

I mean, I wasn't going to be a nurse. I have no domestic skills really. I have no secretarial skills.

My environment never really suggested to me a 'calling' about where I should be going.

Now, I can share with you, how I did figure out where that was eventually, if you would like to hear it?

RDY: Oh, of course.

LM: When I was in the seventh grade, one of our class assignments was to give a speech.

My teacher was named Mrs. Lane. I was a very disruptive kid. Because, I was very bored in school. So, I got up and I made a speech about horses.

At the end of the speech, my teacher stood in the back of the room, and she was silent for about 30 seconds.

Then, finally, she actually blurted out, "Oh, my, you actually do something well."

It was hilarious. Everybody burst out laughing.

I really excelled. Because, I had such passion for horses.

Now, in high school, there were a number of speaking contests and things. I won them all. It never occurred to me, because there were no role models about female speakers…

I never heard of a female speaker. I mean, what speakers did you see in that time other than, maybe your ministers, who weren't female? Maybe your teachers.

But, I knew I wasn't going to be a High School teacher.

So, it didn't occur to me that that was an actual role that I was just born to do. This is something I am very natural at.

My nick name as a kid was 'Motor Mouth'. I talked all the time and I talked about everything.

So, when I look back at my life, there were always hints.

I talk about this a lot in my book *Success Is an Inside Job*. There's a whole chapter about how to look for hints in your life of things that you've done where you are naturally talented. Because, Rachel, I have to tell you, if you really want to be a millionaire, you have to capitalize on your natural talents!

You cannot force yourself to be doing things for money. You have to tap into those 'Natural Abilities' to really exceed in life.

And, when you try to do something, or be someone that you're really not, it may work for a little while. But, it will never actually be big time for you.

RDY: Wow. That's it exactly. I absolutely couldn't agree more!

Now, you said something interesting…You talked about the difference between doing what you love, and working for money. And I want to go back to the farm one more time…

Growing up in that situation, from personal experience, the only houses I could see from my grandmother's farm, and then my dad's farm, were trailers.

When thinking about money, when you started to become successful, did you struggle with an issue of deserving the money that you were getting, or with wealth attraction when you were starting out?

How did you know that you were worth more than that farm? Was there like a defining moment?

LM: Actually, I don't remember a 'Defining Moment'.

My first job... I worked in a little *Tastee Freeze* when I was 16. I worked in a little department store as a roving sales person.

I did lots of little part-time jobs in High School. When I got out of High School, I was this Rock & Roll disc jockey. Then, the same radio station pulled me into sales.

Once I got into sales, I have to tell you, I knew I had found my talent. Because, I sold more the first week in sales, than anybody who had been working there.

I sold it out of pure enthusiasm!

When I started getting paychecks, I was just stunned that I could earn this kind of money.

I knew that I was out there, and I had this work ethic, and I was working hard.

So, when I got my paychecks, I really felt like I earned those paychecks.

So, I don't remember having an *unworthiness process* to the childhood.

As time has gone by in my life, I can remember segments of my life where when I first started to become a professional speaker, I went through what you're talking about. Like, how much to charge, etc.

As a matter of fact, the first real speech that I gave for a local telephone company, I charged $300, and I almost didn't get hired. And this woman gave me a very important lesson.

She said to me, "You charge so little, I didn't think you could be very good."

When she said this to me, Rachel, everything in my whole body started screaming that she was absolutely right! If I didn't believe I had more than $300 worth to contribute to the audience, then I didn't really deserve to be a speaker.

So, I raised my fee to a point that I was afraid to quote it! But, I actually got more work!

I have found now that the world perceives that, the more you charge, the more worthy you are! Provided that you actually *live up* to the billing!

You know, there are people out there who charge outrageous sums who don't actually give outrageous returns for the dollar. I call those people fakes.

If I promise you something, I'm not only going to give you everything I promised, I'm going to give you a lot more than I ever advertised!

So, my motto in business, and one of the reasons I really have become very successful in life is because:

1)   I have high integrity. I am always on time. If I promise you something, I will move heaven and earth and mountains to get it there on time.
2)   I will do an exceptional job and I will give you much more than you ever anticipated for our bargain.

So, I'm a good business bet.

RDY: That is really interesting. Because, I remember when I first started copywriting on my first project that I got hired for, the client paid, and my husband made the comment, "Wow, you just made more in one week than your dad and two brother-in-laws made this entire month!"

And I sabotaged myself and I lost everything...

LM: You did?

RDY: Yeah. In my mind, I was thinking, 'How in the world could I be worth more than my father?' Who I had on this immense pedestal.

So, I struggled for many, many years with an issue of *Deservingness*. So, I was very interested to hear your take on it…

LM: Well, I can tell you. I have a little slight perception about this. See, I did not have my father on a pedestal.

From a very young age, I was very amazed that my father was a bad business man.

He was a great farmer. He was a man of nature. But, he was like living in the wrong era of time.

You see, he would have done really well in the 1800s. Are you with me?

See, he was not a man of his time. It's a long story about my dad. But, he was orphaned at seven years old and had no where to live. I mean, it was a really sad story.

But, he just made very bad business decisions.

I mean, I really was aware when I was growing up that my father bought high and sold low.

We were so poor, we were so struggling.

I remember the nights that I used to hear my parents talking about how they were about to lose the farm.

They didn't know where money was coming from. It was severe.

I mean, I wore second hand clothes. I could never be anything in high school. I could never be a cheer leader. I could never be, you know, on the baton squad.

I couldn't do squat. Because, we had no money. There was no money for the uniforms.

So, I couldn't participate in any of those things.

I remember in high school, one time somebody said, "Why do you always wear the same clothes?"

And I was thinking to myself, 'What are you talking about? These are the only clothes I have.'

So, you know… It just fascinated me that when I was growing up, somehow I was born with an instinct for business.

I absolutely have an ability that I was born with about understanding business.

Now, I did not inherit this from my family. I can assure you.

I didn't get it from my environment.

I don't how to explain this. But, I have an instinct of understanding, for lack of better word, business.

I just understand it. I understand what you need to do. I understand how to negotiate for it. I understand how to present yourself with it.

So, instead of my environment showing me how to do it… I will tell you from my therapist that one thing my parents did was show me how *not to do it.*

Remember, we choose 'roles' in life. So, I chose just not to follow them.

I didn't know who I was going to follow. But, it certainly wasn't going to be them.

RDY: Now, it's interesting that you brought up 'following someone'. Because I do less speaking and more copywriting,..

But, there have been times when I've been on stage, I've heard this 'Glass Ceiling' comment being used over and over again.

About how, *'Because you're a woman, you're never going to sell more than X amount…*

You're never going to be able to send more than so many people to the back of the room. Your pitches are never going to be better than the man who spoke before you.'
Do you buy into the whole 'Glass Ceiling' idea for women?

LM: Well, if I can just be very blunt here...

RDY: Go for it.

LM: I have one word for that. Are you ready?

RDY: Yeah.

LM: Bullshit.

Bullshit, bullshit, and more bullshit.

I have heard all the stuff, Rachel. You have to choose what you want to believe in life. This is one that I know you are doing this book for. You know, primarily women. It's nice if men read it. But, let me just tell you something…

Women have been programmed in a way. It's a control program. And I grew up such a little renegade, rebel, untamed girl. That when people tell me I can't do something, there's a little fire cracker that goes off inside of me that basically says, "Watch me. How dare you tell me my limitations!"

And, if anything irks me more, upsets me, or ticks me off more, it's some man telling me that 'Because I'm a female, that I can't do something you can do.'

Bullshit! I can do anything I put my mind to! I'm as smart as you! I'm not going to say 'I can go out and pick up some 300 pound thing.' I'm not that crazy. I don't want to be a rocket scientist. I don't want to be a brain surgeon. I want to do what I do using *my* talents.

So, just so you know, Rachel, when people talk about that stuff, I have sold as much as 750,000 dollars worth of stuff in 90 minutes by my little stuff. So, I don't believe any of that.

RDY: That's the kind of answer I was hoping you were going to give!

LM: I mean, seriously... I get so riled up about people putting limitations on other people about what you can or can't do.

And there are people who I'm dear friends with and who are very, very big in this industry, who preach this on a regular basis. And I have stood in the back of the room in seminars after they have said it and yelled out, "Bullshit. Ladies in the room don't believe any of that! You can buy into it if you want to... "

I spoke with Marlo Thomas a number of years ago. And, in her speech, she said her father said to her one time, "Put on your own blinders, like you do horses, and run your own race."

I took that advice very seriously!
I run my own race. And there are days I'm going to be great, and sell a lot, and there are going to be days I only do OK.

But, just because I'm a female I'm not going to allow other people to prejudice, other people's narrow view of reality, their own limitations of seeing potential and talent affect who I am.

I can tell you that in my life I have allowed people to do that and I immediately start to ask myself, "Whose life is this?

This is my life!

I'm not here to impress them. I'm not here to prove that women are better or anything. I'm here to run my own race. And anybody who's listening to my words, let me tell you..."

When I do female seminars, I really cut no slack.

Every woman has to decide that this is her race, and that what other people think is none of your business. That is just their thoughts.

The only thoughts that really count to you are YOUR thoughts about YOURSELF! Because, we are self-fulfilling prophecies.

If you believe in their limitations, you will experience them.

I just don't want to buy into that. I've got a short life and I'm going to ride it screaming as loud as I can through it. **RDY**: Exactly. I've got a sentence that I use whenever I have had a bad day... If I think in my head, "Oh, well. No one would blame you if you didn't finish XYZ." Or, "If you didn't do XYZ, then...." If I think that in my head, that tells me more than anything I need to finish, that I need to do, or whatever it is that I'm working on.

If I can say, "No one would blame you if you didn't do this," then that's all the more reason that it needs to get done!

LM: Absolutely. Absolutely.

RDY: So now, as women, you were talking about programming before. We are often taught - I prefer to even say pre-programmed to be a little more docile and not necessarily assertive...

Would you say that there's such a thing as a successful business woman who isn't aggressive and tenacious?

LM: There might be. I don't know any. You know, I'm from the south... I live in Virginia Beach, Virginia.

And of course I *do* consider myself a 'Southern Woman'. And I like being a southern woman. I like being gracious. I like being elegant.

But, when people meet me, I have this blonde hair, and I'm a southern woman. So, they sort of get the wrong impression about me.

They're kind of looking at you thinking they know you. But, after like two minutes of talking to me, there's really like a gladiator behind all this. Behind this, you know, southern woman thing.

I don't think you can be successful in life if you aren't aggressive about going for what you want.

I don't think you can ever be successful without being tenacious about what you want. Because no one goes out and becomes a success overnight! That's a fallacy.

You know, the old joke, I'm a '20-year overnight success'. That is so true in life! Everybody I know, everybody I've ever studied, has lots of failures. And, we should really rejoice in our failures. You know, afterwards.

Because, we can see that if you didn't learn that lesson, whatever that lesson was, there's going to be opportunities that come to you in the future that you wouldn't be able to be successful at if you had not learned that important lesson that you learned in failure.

All of my so called 'Failures' in life actually became my greatest gifts! They didn't look like gifts at the time, I might add. But, they *were* gifts.

When we use the word 'Aggressive', I'm sure you mean 'Aggressive towards what you're going for'?

RDY: Yes.

LM: Because when we're aggressive towards other people, I don't think that works. I don't think it works for men or women.

But, when we're aggressive towards what we want to create in life, you see…Ultimately, what we are, are 'Manifesters'.

And some people who look at life, look at it as if life is going to give you something.

I look at life as... Here is this big Toy Store, and I have to decide what toys I want to play with.

So, I actively, aggressively go towards what I want. And I have to be very tenacious about it. Because there are so many times in my life where everybody told me I couldn't do something.

They told me, "You will never be able to be a professional speaker." Well, we'll see about that!

Or, you know, "How are you going to become an author? Because, who cares what you have to say? You're just a southern woman."

Yeah, well, we'll see about that, too!

I was told when I decided to get into television, "You have no background in television. Who is ever going to hire you?"

Well, I proved all of these things wrong.

Anybody who wants to be super successful, you have to realize that you probably have more ambition than time and that's good.

So, we are put on earth to be creators. We are put on earth to be creating things, and manifesting things, and enjoying life, and actively pursuing what you want instead of waiting for it to come to you.

So, I don't know anybody who literally becomes successful without continuously baby-stepping towards something.

Success is not some straight line, Rachel. And I know you... we all know this...Some people see 'Success' as some straight line. Success is this very crooked, jagged chart.

You know, you succeed a little bit. Then, a couple of bad things happen. You kind of fall back a little bit, then regroup. And if you're not failing at things, then you're not really stretching yourself!

The difference is, as Henry Ford said, "If you think you can, or you think you cannot, you're right."

The truth is that, you have to be stretching yourself, breaking through boundaries, trying new things, and having fun with the whole adventure. It's an adventure!

See, life is an adventure. And, if you see it as this adventure, then you don't take it all so seriously.

Your life is a story and in everybody's story there's ups, there's downs, there's tragedy, there's, you know, triumph. There's everything.

So, your life is a story and anybody who has this neutral story, how boring can that be? I want to go through life just really enjoying the whole process, you know? I'm going through riding at a gallop!

RDY: Now, ok, you've mentioned several times the television, and speaking on stage, and I know from having seen it personally, you shared the stage with more influential people just in the past five years than some people will meet in an entire lifetime!

Do you ever get star struck?

LM: Sure, absolutely! That is part of the fun of it. Sure.

RDY: Was it intimidating at first? I mean, we're talking people like Tony Robbins, and others, that some folks could barely dream of even being in the audience with some of these folks, and you're up on stage with them!

LM: Am I intimidated by them? Absolutely not. Because, once you get to know these people, no matter who they are... Let me give you a little story.

How I actually became a professional speaker is, I was at a very down time in my life where I had gotten divorced. I left my business that I had started with him. And I was just in this in-between time working in commercial real estate. Which I have to tell you, was *not* my idea of a good time!

LM: I went to... Actually I got dragged to an American rally that was one of these huge rallies. It had Art Linkletter, and Zig Ziglar in it.

I'm sitting in the audience. I'm in a very bad mood. I didn't want to be there. You know, if you're in a bad mood you like to stay in a bad mood...

But, I got listening to Zig Ziglar, and Art Linkletter, and all these great speakers. And, I had truly a vision! I've never had anything like this in my entire life, before it, or since it.

But, I saw myself on stage with Zig Ziglar. I literally had this vision of myself on stage with Zig Ziglar, and it absolutely scared me!

So, I went home and I had to go to bed. I was like, "What the heck does this mean?"

So, over the next few months, what happened was, I actually realized that was my destiny!

So, once I decided to become a professional speaker I... and, by the way, just so you know, my preparations for becoming a professional speaker is I went and had cards printed and suddenly I'm a professional speaker.

So, I started visualizing myself every single night on stage with Zig Ziglar, and it took a mere 13 years. But, one day, on a Sunday afternoon, the phone rang.

I get this phone call from a promoter who was promoting Zig Ziglar who said, "We've heard about you, Lee Milteer. And we would like for you to join our tour."

Now, I had never made an application towards them. I never called them. I never sent them a letter. I never did anything. They called me out of the blue.

I went on tour with Zig Ziglar and then ended up working with Art Linkletter too!

But, what happened to me because of that particular thing, and the reason I'm not intimidated by people, is because once I got to know these people, they all had their own stories of how they got there.

None of these very famous people, none of them...

I got to speak with the late Dr. Norman Vincent Peale. I got to speak and tour with Og Mandino. I mean, some of the most famous people of our lifetime!

How did I do that? I decided, in advance, that I wanted to be on stage with these people! I visualized myself on stage with them, and then I allowed the universe to do its natural thing, and attract the circumstances where I would be on stage with these people!

So, when I finally do meet them, Rachel, I've already seen them in my head. I've already had conversations with them. I already feel like an equal. I already feel privileged to be on the stage with them. I have pre-lived that experience prior to it physically happening.

RDY: I felt that way the first time I met Zig, as well! I had butterflies in my stomach. But, it wasn't because, "Oh, I can't believe I am in the same room with Zig," because I got to meet him at his office.

It was "I feel like you're my friend. I have so many things I want to share with you. Because I feel like we're just friends that haven't spoken in a long time."

LM: Exactly. When I was on tour with Zig, I used to have breakfast with him. And, you know, we never really talked about business very much. I mean we talked about everything.

It was like someone I had known. You know, he was sort of like a grandfather figure.

It was someone I had known for a very long time. And, by the way, it was very daunting to go on stage after Zig Ziglar.

RDY: I can imagine!

LM: Oh, my gosh. It was just like "What the hell? Can I go on stage *before* Zig Ziglar?"

But, you know, sometimes I did go on before. Sometimes I went on afterwards. I preferred the before thing. But, you have to be damn good.

So, everybody that I've ever met who are these great famous people. I'm very honored to meet them. But, I have this appreciation that they all got there, because they worked really hard to be there! There's a lot of sacrifice to success that nobody sees behind the scenes.

You know, I traveled to 100 cities a year for six straight years doing public seminars.

If you're going to be good on stage, you would be good after that!

I mean, I did all my due diligence. I paid my dues. And everybody I've ever met who has been on stages like that, has really paid their dues.

RDY: Now, I've noticed through the course of our conversation that there's one word that appears more than anything else that we've said and it is, "I".

It sounds like a lot of the success you've achieved has come from within. And I know you talk about *'Mastering Yourself'*. What does that mean?

LM: Well, I did create my success. Everybody creates their own success! *'Mastering Yourself'* means that you're willing to do the work within…To work on your Self Esteem, to work on your Self Image, to work on your Self Worth.

You can never go any further in life than you give yourself permission to go. We are Self-Fulfilling Prophecies!

I take this to women all the time. You know, it's nice to get accolades from the outside world. But, the only thing that really counts is when you look in the mirror.

I had a conversation yesterday with Dan Kennedy about that. This year I have done 'Millionaire Smarts', which is my big coaching program for other coaches, for 6 straight years.

It's been 72 months of like writing a book every month, straight! Never repeated, never flaked out, never have been a day late!

He said to me, "Well, you know, the whole world won't know that."

I said, "It doesn't make any difference! I know it. I am proud of myself!" You know, I don't need to advertise it. It's no big deal to anybody else.

Who cares? I care.

So, what you're asking me is "How do you get to the I?" Is that the question?

RDY: Yeah.

LM: All right, remember my background was that females weren't valued…

In your life there are always challenges that are presented to you, that are really the keys to your success. The challenge that is presented to each human being is, the challenge brings out the greatness. So, the challenge I had was, females were not acknowledged, females were not appreciated, females were not valued.

So, what did I do?

I worked harder, stronger, took more risk. I did 10 times more than everybody else was doing! So, there *was* some need within me, when I was younger, to prove that I was good enough. Now, I didn't know that I was doing that. But, that's actually what I was doing. And now there is still that need.

Every person I've ever met, who has been really successful, has pushed themselves harder, because they want, in some ways, to prove themselves.

As I think I said to you earlier, every successful person is very insecure and that is one of the reasons they've become successful.

So, instead of seeing it as a detriment, see it as an attribute that you can utilize. That inspires you. Motivates you to go out there and do a little bit more than the average person does.

So, everything really is about yourself. The one part of yourself, which, you're never supposed to talk about yourself, you are never supposed to brag.

But, women have just been so programmed to down play their success your whole life.

If you really want to... since this book is about being a millionaire, if you really want to be a millionaire, you have to go past what other people think...

Into *'I'm willing to love myself. I'm a unique being. I was born and raised in different environments, different social, economic, educational backgrounds than everybody else. I am totally unique.'*

There's no one like you in the entire universe. Why not celebrate that verses compare yourself to other people?

I have a program with Peak Performers. And, one of the things that I share with all the Peak Performers is that, as entrepreneurs, we have this disease of comparing ourselves to other people.

And there is always going to be someone taller, makes more money, more handsome, more beautiful, getting more PR. You know, whatever.

There's always going to be someone who is at the top of the heap at the moment.

That doesn't detract from you. It doesn't take away from you. It doesn't make this any less for you.

They are living their life. Let's celebrate them. Be happy for them…But, also honor *yourself*!

You are at the right time, at the right place, where you are, at this second, learning your *own* life lessons! This is *your* adventure! This is *your* life's story!

If you would write it all down, the whole world is listening. They are reading *your* story! They're not comparing your story to somebody else. So, I encourage women to honor the uniqueness of their contribution.

RDY: Now, to the women who are reading this right now, a lot of them going through... trying to find balance between when they're at work, they have mommy guilt, because they're not at home with the kids. Or, they're trying to find a balance between social life and running their own business.

And you seem to be getting it all done in a day. You know, you're a wife, an entrepreneur, you still have a social life. How do you find that balance?

LM: Well, I have a lot of help. I'm a big believer in being the leader. And, when I say that, meaning *my* job in life is to earn the income to be the provider for many other people.

So, I have three assistants. I have a housekeeper. My husband works in my business. He takes care of me. I have surrounded myself with support teams.

I'm not going to say the average person can do this. But, I didn't start like this. I started all by myself. I was a terrible secretary to myself. I was horrible. I realized in the first three months, that I went into business for myself, that if I had to do the books, the bookkeeping, if I had to clean the house, if I had to do all this other stuff, I was going to fail.

You only have 1440 minutes per day.

So, what I do is I have really honed my world into: What does Lee Milteer do the best? And I do that.

I oversee a lot of other things. But, I'm a great delegator! Remember, I started leading people at 12 years old. I realized that you, as a single individual, can never acquire, manufacture, manifest reality unless you have a team of people who work on your behalf. No one becomes successful alone. It is impossible. There are not enough hours in the day.

How do I create a balance is, I have very strong boundaries between what I will and will not do. I don't accept every invitation. I have a very limited social life, by the way. Because, I'm not a social person. Most of my energy is very expended into my work, because my work is my life. This is my destiny. This is what I choose. This is what I like to do. I'm not a person who likes to go to cocktail parties and talk about the weather. I find that boring. I don't like it.

I *will* make an appearance when necessary. I can be social. I like people. But, I really honor that I need more down time, quiet time. Because I'm a creator. I'm a writer. I have to create things. You only have so much mental, physical, emotional, spiritual, and financial energy.

So, here is how you balance yourself:

You take those five energies and you decide how much time that you can give to those energies. You create huge boundaries around yourself, and you make decisions, and you make choices of where you are going to spend your energy.

Now, I want to tell you, I have no children. All my children have four legs and fur, ok? So, that was a decision I made a long time ago.

It wouldn't be fair for me to bring children in on this earth plane when I'm gone to 100 cities a year. That's not right. It would be wrong for me to try to bring a child into this earth without the proper nutrition, care, and love to be there.

So, I made this decision and that was the right decision for me.

So, by the way, success is a lifetime thing, Rachel.

You know, we have segments of our life where you're devoting yourself to your children, the most important thing in life, your children. You know, it's all of us making these decisions about what our priorities are.

So, I cannot be a social butterfly *and* be a great success in writing, in traveling, and speaking. I just can't do it. I don't know anybody who can. So, the balance has to be what do you want to let into your reality ,and what is not necessary?

So, for instance, I never watch the news. I don't spend any time with the news. I barely look at the newspaper. I am pretty much reading the comics and look at the coupons, ok. But, I don't allow myself to spend time in realities that are not beneficial to me. I don't spend time with people who depress me or who think average.

So, for all of us who want to be successful, you have to realize: analyze who, and what, are beneficial to you. Who, and what, are not beneficial to you.

You must create this knowledge for yourself.

And, once you have that, it's very easy to say 'No' with love and kindness to things, people, situations that aren't really beneficial.

Now, I want to share with you one question you haven't asked me, that is very important for women.

RDY: Ok.

LM: The word obligation. Obligation is a very, very serious thing. And most women and men do a lot of things in life out of what they perceive as obligation. Right?

Now, we're not talking about kids, here, ok? But, the obligation of being on some committee, or the obligation of someone has done something for you, or something nice, and now you have to do something in return.

Whenever you do something out of obligation, what happens is, you're not really in integrity with yourself.

Because if you *want* to do it that's great. But, if you really, really, really, really *don't* want to do it, and you do it anyway, it takes a big toll on yourself. So, we all do things out of obligation from time to time that we have to do.

But, I just want to warn you. Don't set up situations where you're always obligated to doing things.

For example, someone said to me recently she was obligated to give some kind of family party.

I said, "Why?"

She said, "Well, you know, her in laws had always done this and now she felt obligated to continue the tradition."

I said, "Well, that's a choice you're making. If you want to do it, you should absolutely do it. But, if you're doing it and you're going to do it from the perspective of you don't really want to do it, but you *have* to do it, then do you understand the different energetics?

When you do something you really don't want to do, it's not in integrity." So, be *very* aware of obligations and choose them carefully.

RDY: And I think that can even extend all the way down into something as simple and mundane as answering your cell phone if you're working on a project.

Like, I don't take incoming calls. And it drives my family crazy.

Because my family and friends think that if they take the time to pick up the phone and call me that I should take the time to answer.

But, as a copywriter, it's very hard to be in the middle of a train of thought, stop, get on the phone, talk about what Uncle June Bug is doing, and then get that train of thought back and start that train moving again.

So... as a result, I don't take incoming calls, and it drives them absolutely batty. But, I don't feel a sense of obligation to answer the phone just because it rings.

LM: Rachel, that's fabulous! And it's a wonderful example! You're 100 percent right!

What I was trying to relay here, just to add to your training...

Because your readers may not be copywriters, so they may not understand... I'm a writer, so I totally understand. You have a thought. The phone rings. Your thought, you know, was vaguely there, and then you got distracted. And it takes you like a half an hour to get back to the thought. But, it's never as good as it was when you first initially had it.

So, I have a little sign on my door when I'm writing. It says, "Do not interrupt me unless the house is on fire."

And, by the way, the wrath of Lee will happen! So, I have really trained people. I'm very big into training people, meaning sharing with people what my perspective and boundaries are.

I say to them, I really appreciate that you may not comprehend my life. And, I apologize in advance, if you don't agree with me. However, this is the way I have to do things. And I just stick to it.

RDY: Well, for a while, I felt guilty. You know, the phone would be sitting there, and it would be ringing, and I would purposely not answer it. And I felt guilty.

So, eventually I got to where I just didn't even turn the ringer on. Then, when it's time for me to check my messages, I'll look and see how many missed calls I have. So, it allows me to focus on the thing that clients pay me to do, and not sit there and feel...

You know, I've seen my mother practically break her leg to get to the phone just because it's ringing. She doesn't even know who's on the other end.

LM: Exactly. Well, this is because you value what you do, and your own creative input. I actually don't accept any social calls during the day, none at all.

You know, there are certain people on my VIP list that my staff will let me know is on the phone. I will take their call. But, they have to be on my VIP list. I just have these great boundaries around myself.

And, if I may add to this, the two useless emotions in life are guilt and worry.

You can't feel guilty enough to change anything and you can't worry enough to change anything. And when you have both of those emotions it's very detrimental to yourself.

And, again, one of the discerning things I have learned about life is to ask myself these questions: What is beneficial for me? And, what is not beneficial for me?

Those two lists help me discern how I should utilize my greatest asset, which is my time. See, one of my missions in life is to share information that allows other people to use their own potential and talents. That is my theme of life. And because it is my theme of life, I mean I actually live that!

I want to be a living embodiment of sharing information with people that assists them in living a much more joyful, productive, successful life!

You know, I'm sharing with you, in the short time that we have been together, Rachel, some things about my life.

The truth is, we all have successes in our lives and we all have tragedy. The choice we have every single day of our life, is to look for what is good and how we can be of service and contribute to life. I believe in whatever you give, the universe gives back to you. So, what you sow, you shall reap.

So, in my life, because I like to give to people, the world gives me so much back! And if I may, I would like to share with your readers that my web site is: Milteer.com

I have a wonderful group of products, books, DVDs, CD systems that have all been designed to help people find joy, find success, find contentment, to find their place and to be able to live their life the way they want to live their life.

I've gone through a lot in my life. I've lived, and had a lot of life experience. And I would like my legacy on earth to be as someone who brought light into the world.

RDY: I will just say, too, that having access to the FREE 'Untamed Successes' letter that you put out has just meant volumes as far as the information that you deliver to your readers. And that's something else great that I got from Milteer.com!

LM: Well, thank you! We work pretty hard to get out that free newsletter. Every once in a while we're going, "wow!"

You know, this is a lot of work each week. So, I wish that everybody remember everything that you read, everything that you are exposed to, everything that you involve in your world affects you.

We should all seek out the books, the educational materials, and be a life time learner. Always be curious in life. Always be adapting to the change in the world.

Because the world right now, Rachel, is changing at light speed. And, if I can say one thing to women it's: Adapt to change. Adapt to change. Adapt to change.

Scan the landscape of your life looking for opportunities where you can use your natural talents, abilities, and skills. To not only share those. But, that you're utilizing that change to your benefit.

Do not fight the change of reality. Embrace it. Love it. And ride the wave.

Make sure you're visualizing what you want in life. Because, when you visualize something, you magnetically attract it to you.

It's no accident, Rachel, that I've achieved where I am today. I just want you to know this… I still feel like I'm just getting started!

RDY: How exciting is that?

LM: I mean, seriously! You look back on your life and you go, "Wow, I have accomplished all these things." But yet, when I wake up in the morning, I'm like, 'I haven't done enough. I've got more to do!'

It's like a little seedling that has just poked itself out of the earth and is looking at the sun going, "Oh, there is so much to be done. There is so much to grow. Life is so filled with opportunities. And I'm going to figure out what they are and go in that direction!

RDY: That is so exciting! SO exciting!

LM: It is. Nobody holds you back in life, but yourself.

RDY: Oh, I couldn't agree more. I couldn't agree more.

LM: So, this book you have *Conversations with Female Millionaires*, any woman who wants to really blossom in life has got to give herself permission to do so.

That's probably the most important thing I have said today. If you really want to be somewhere, give yourself permission to be there.

RDY: And that's the *one* thing I wish I had realized back when I was just starting out and struggling with that issue of deservedness. I felt like someone else needed to give me permission when I had the permission all along!

LM: If you look at all the messages in our reality. *The Wizard of Oz*, the movie where you already have the red slippers and you just click your heels.

I mean, there are messages in movies. There are messages in books.

There are messages everywhere, that it's only us that needs to give ourselves permission for that. Just so you know, Rachel, I often experienced the same thing about going to the next level in my life.

We have that internal conversation about 'Who am I to do that?' Am I delusionary? But, ultimately, and I might get a little metaphysical here... But, ultimately we all live in our own world, which is our head. And we have to see ourselves in that position before we can actually physically get there.

So, in all my books, *Spiritual Power Tools for Successful Selling, Success is an Inside Job*, and all my many, many programs in life…

The one thing I always say is we are '*Self-Fulfilling Prophecies.*'

So, envision what you want in the most realistic manner. Hold the vision. Look for evidence. Keep going in that direction and just know that this is your adventure.

It really *is* all going to work out. Even if you go in a direction, and it doesn't work out, it's just the old saying, 'a door closes, another window opens'.

The other thing I always like to remind people… *You always land on your feet!* No matter how many times you fall down, you land on your feet. You get up again, and you spring board into the next thing.

I did public seminars for women for six straight years. I did over 600 seminars for just women.

And why they liked me is…I was such a rebel. I dared their limitations. I pushed their buttons about things like *How dare you believe that you can do that.* Who says you *can't* do that? Why are you believing that?

And when bad things happen, so what? You know, somebody criticizes you. So what? So you failed at something? So what? Pick yourself up, dust yourself off, move on.

It's all this *permission* in life that women wait for from men, and the outside world, and I want to equate this to... I see so many women thinking, *'Well, what will other people think?'*

When you go dancing and you're out on the dance floor and everybody is dancing. Everybody is so concerned about how they're dancing. They're really not paying attention to how other people are dancing. They don't care.

It's sort of like life. If you realized how little other people are actually thinking about you, you wouldn't take it so seriously.

RDY: Exactly. That reminds me of when my husband and I first got started. We went from living in our car, to living in a friend's basement for a while, and then I started creating my own information products.

I remember at one point going to the guy that I was working for and saying, "You know, you're this prestigious real estate investment guru guy.

I've written this home study course on marketing and it is just for Real Estate investors.

I've already done all the work, if you would just allow me to put your name on it too. Because I'm a nobody right now. If you would do that... You know, I really think it will take off."

And I will never forget him looking at me and saying, "You really think you can write a home study course?" And that was all it took.

LM: Good...

RDY: From then on I said, "Never again will I be under the thumb, or obligated to somebody thinking that I'm not good enough to do it all by myself!"

LM: That was a real gift to you. I look at life, and sometimes there are 'Earth Angels'. And if women would look at messages they get like that from a positive view, like you did, that he gave you a great gift, then all of us would be much better off.

There are gifts everywhere and sometimes the gifts are bad things. But, it's just how you decide to interpret it, how to take that information and make it work for you.

Our whole society right now is portraying women in a very negative light.

You know, you're supposed to be young. You're supposed to dress sexy. You're supposed to be this pampered female.

There are female 'gurus' out there today who are selling a real bill of goods to women that you have to dress like a hooker. You have to flitter around and be at all the parties and you have to do all this stuff. Very unrealistic and it's not working.

You know, listen to your heart more about reality.

You asked me a question earlier, about a lot of people I was on stage with. There's a lot of people in our world who portray one thing, but are not that.

So, listen to your heart about who tells you the truth. Because your intuition and your heart can always tell you, if you listen, who is telling the truth and who is not. So there are false prophets.

RDY: Most definitely, yes. The guy that said that to me, once I got a look at the way he would say one thing from stage, and then he ran his business a completely different way off stage. He was convincing the people in the audience, 'Hey, this is the way to do it.' And was getting paid very handsomely for it.

LM: Exactly. It was very disillusioning to me when I realized that people were saying things from the platform, or in books, or in educational systems, but they weren't living it. They were just selling it. Eventually I always feel that the false prophets will be exposed.

I'm very careful to put things into perspective. Just because it's all glittery and gold does not mean that's really what it is. I'm very careful to listen to my inner wisdom. I'm a very spiritual woman. And I really do honor that instinctual, intuition part of myself.

Where if I hear something, but it doesn't set right with me. I'm very reluctant to follow someone's advice on face value only. It has to feel right for me. And I'm a little disturbed by some messages that are being given to women that you can get ahead without working hard. Or, if you just dress the part, look the part and act the part, you can get ahead.

Well, maybe for a short time. But, there has to be some legitimate information, work, or contribution to really be successful.

RDY: Because eventually you'll say or do something if you're just looking the part, that someone will go, "Wait, what?"

LM: Well, eventually people's real self will show and when you have confidence that you're connected to something bigger than yourself, when you have that connection, that inner spiritual connection, you don't just look at the physical world. You really access another dimension of, does this resonate with you? Does it feel true?

And that was the biggest shock to me when I went into this business. Some of the people who portrayed themselves to be certain things were just illusions. And, by the way, most of those people have disappeared.

RDY: Yeah, and that's actually one of the things that got me into the public speaking side. My father is a minister, and I would see him speak from stage literally every Sunday. He has mastered the art of the pitch. He pitched Jesus. I mean, not to in any way that sounds sacrilegious.

LM: Right. I know exactly what you're saying.

RDY: You know, when he did the altar call at the end and said, "Do you want to come forward?"

That's what that equated to me when I started going to these seminars and seeing the way that people pitched. And the emotion that they were drawing from their audience was the same emotion that my dad drew out of his congregation.

And, just like you send people to the back of the room to buy the thing that you know is going to revolutionize their business, if they will just, you know, open the Saran wrap. He would promote the offering plate to be able to better the church, to give them a better experience every time they walked through the doors on a Sunday.

So, seeing that made me say, 'You know, he does it every single Sunday. How hard can it be?' So, the first time I got on stage I went, "Oh, wow. This is not the same at all."

LM: Right.

RDY: This is a lot harder than I thought!

LM: I do want to share with you. I try to never use the word 'sell'. I use the word 'invest'. Because, if I'm trying to sell somebody something, it sort of shuts me down. But, if I think of, 'I would like for you to invest in yourself', then it opens my heart.

RDY: That's interesting. Because I heard Tom Hopkins say that from stage and I always thought of it from the customer's perspective. That they would feel better hearing 'invest' rather than sell.

I never thought about it from my own perspective though. That makes a lot of sense.

LM: Well, let's just go a little deeper here…Everything in your life is a reflection of who you are inside.

So, if you're getting a lot of problems on the outside of your world…

If you're getting rejection, you're getting whatever problems you have in the inside of yourself are being mirrored in the outside world.

So, the real secret of success is that when you said, 'I' a while ago, I didn't go into this. But, you really have to clean up your own act to be in such integrity with yourself that you're vibrating such integrity. Because then when people are listening to you they're attracted to what you're sharing.

So, you're not ramming it down their throat. You're not 'selling it' to them. You're offering an opportunity for them to invest in their own future.

When I'm in that state of mind on stage, I'm not really concerned about who is going to the back of the room to fill out forms. I know I am just being a servant.

And, if they decide to invest, that's fantastic. If they decide not to invest that's their choice. I'm very neutral about it. I have to become very, very neutral about the whole process. If I'm attached to the end results, it will hinder the end results. I do my best and let it go. That is all I can do.

RDY: Do you ever feel like if you didn't sell enough, that you didn't do your job in communicating to them exactly how much better their business, their life, their *insert whatever it is here* would be if they did buy?

LM: Everybody has those feelings. But, I just want to share with you from my background…

I came up as a professional speaker first. Where the first five years of my speaking life, I never pitched anything. I just did speeches.

So, selling wasn't my priority. My priority was to give a speech that changed somebody's life.

So, what I was really trying to do was to get them to invest in a different way of thinking.

Then I got into the world of platform sales and there would be times I would get off the stage and the promoter is yelling at everybody who was on stage saying "We didn't sell enough!"

And there was this feeling of failure all of us would have at the same time. That we had let down the promoter. Where the truth is we did the best we could.

You know, a lot of successful people have days where they bomb. Meaning you're at the wrong audience, at the wrong time. Or, there are environmental factors that affect people. The news affects people. There's a million contributors to how you financially sell on any specific day.
And, if you base your *Sense of Worth* on just one performance, you're doing yourself a great disservice.

Some days you might write brilliant things Rachel. Then, the next day you read it and go, "Hmmm."

RDY: What was I thinking?

LM: I need to hit the delete button on all of that and start all over again.

RDY: Yeah.

LM: Because I've had a million failures. But, then I would look back the next day and go, "Ok. Where was the little bug a boo?"

Well, here's the most important question you can ask yourself: "How can I do this better next time?" Not beat yourself up because you were a failure. Not everybody is meant to be a platform sales person.

And there's a lot of people trying to be platform sales people who should not be platform sales people. There's a pressure. There's this false reality.

Let me tell you… I'm *so* happy to go do a speech somewhere where I don't have to pitch anything!

It's such a relief. It's such a joy to get back to my true purpose. You know, you have to do it to make a living in our world.

I enjoy those speeches. I love free speeches where I can say anything I want. Because I don't really care what people will think.

So, I do a lot of free speeches for charities and things. And I'm like a wild woman. Because I'm having a ball.
But, you know… Go out there and love yourself!

It's not always about these techniques. Everything is about feeling! Everything is about feeling. So, you can feel crappy and say all the right things and get no results...

Because, only 7% of communications is the words. 93% is different energetics.

RDY: When I started speaking, I was 90 pounds heavier. I always blamed the fact that I may not have been able to send as many people to the back of the room on, "Oh, well, I didn't master the art of the pitch well enough." Or, "Well, it was just a bad audience." Or, "The guy before me sold 75 percent of the room! How was I going to top that?"

When, in reality, it was because my outward appearance looked like I had *'checked out on life.'*

Because, I was over 200 pounds. And inside myself, I felt like crap, because I looked like crap on the outside.

So, I had this tug of war going on within me. And that was what was translating over to the audience more so than any of the words that I said.

LM: Oh, Rachel! If you wrote a book on that particular thing, it would be a wild Best Seller! You could call it *"Excuses."* That's the name of the book. *Excuses,* because this is what our society is programmed for!
What's your excuse?

See, you've seen me on stage, and I sincerely hope I come across as a person who is talking from the heart.

RDY: Oh, absolutely.

LM: I don't want you to blow my horn here. But, there's not a lot of that up there on stages. There are people who don't appreciate that, by the way. A lot of them!

They just want the techniques. They are very *Lower Consciousness* people.

I've learned to accept that. There's people who don't like the 'Right Thinking' type stuff. Or the 'Feeling' stuff. They just want the techniques.

They're very lower consciousness people. They're not my audience.

My audience is really pretty much *High Conscious* people. I can't be a whole pie. I can only be a slice in the pie.

So, who you are is actually more important than what you say. That's why the "I" is so important.

RDY: Yeah. Because, and especially for women…We're constantly guilted into – there's that word again - into taking care of everybody else. We're supposed to come last, because that's what we're supposed to do.

LM: We're supposed to be the cheer leaders, the nurturers, of everybody else.

RDY: Yes. It was actually seeing a picture of myself and Bill Glazer. Because, Dan Kennedy was what gave me the motivation to get out of that basement situation. The first event that I went to was the one where Dan broke his back.

I was so looking forward to being able to just shake Dan's hand. I mean, I had tears in my eyes when they introduced him on stage. Because, all the years of everything that I had been through to get to that point all came rushing back at the same time!

So, at the end of the event, I had my picture taken with Bill. Because, obviously, Dan was out of commission.

I got the picture back. (Someone else had taken it for me.) I looked at it and went, "Oh, my, *THAT'S* the appearance I'm giving to one of the two men that I feel assisted me in getting out? I'm showing my gratitude by looking like this?"

So, I felt like the appearance I gave to everyone else, whether it was influential mentors or my next customer, was "Yeah, I really don't give a crap about myself. So, I wouldn't expect you to give a crap about me either."

That was what launched me into losing the 70 pounds was just that picture with Bill. Because I had spent so many years taking care of everybody else but me.

LM: I'm very serious of encouraging you to consider a book on your own about this.

Maybe interviewing other women, or men too, who have experienced what I call 'Self-Limitation', lack of self-worth.

You know, how that affects you in the world and how easy it is to have excuses and be in denial about that.

By the way, in my program *"Overcoming Unproductive Behaviors"*, I deal with that almost exclusively in the sense of: we do things to soothe ourselves to distract ourselves from our own pain. Whether it's smoking, shopping, eating.

Whatever your little addiction is at the moment that distracts you from the pain you're feeling. Because it's 'Unworthiness'. So, I'm very proud of you. Congratulations!

RDY: There have been a lot of tears shed over the past six years. I will say that!

LM: Look. I don't know anybody who goes through life without tragedy. I've had terrible tragedy in my life. My husband got killed on Christmas Eve. My story is so wild. But, you don't dare share all of it on stage. People would be, you know, weeping.

You can't have the joy without the sadness. Everything is the Yin and the Yang.

RDY: Well, the sadness is what gives you the appreciation for the joy when it comes.

LM: Yes. And, you know, that sucks, doesn't it?

RDY: Yes, it does.

LM: I always go, "Well, this just sucks." And people ask me all the time. They say, "Do you ever get depressed?"

Oh, my. Yes. I get depressed. I mean, when people get on stage, Rachel, and say they're never depressed. All I can say is, "What bullshit that is!"

Who the hell doesn't get depressed?

RDY: No kidding.

LM: It's like, "What kind of drugs are you on? Send *me* some! " But, there's so much illusion in this world. There are so many people selling such loads of crap. I have real issue with sometimes not just screaming at people. "You can't be serious following this person, can you?"

I mean, are you really this brain dead? But, you know, they're easily led. Because the illusion looks attractive.

RDY: It's funny... I've been writing a book chronicling my weight loss and I called it, *'What if you were Thin?'*

LM: Oh, great title.

RDY: Oh, thank you. Because, that was a thought that never occurred to me.

But, after I saw that picture with Bill, I said, "Oh, my! I have *got* to do something! I have got to radically change my life!"

I smoked 2 packs a day, ate anything that was close enough to get my hand on and put it in my mouth, because it was very soothing to me to eat rather than to...

LM: Feel.

RDY: Yes. Because, I was still dealing with issues of self-worth. You know, my dad is a pastor. How can I possibly make more money than him? You know? Even up until the past three years. It was very difficult.

Once I finally mastered that, the weight started coming off. I was looking at myself in the mirror and not continuing to see 210 pounds.

LM: Well, while we've done this interview I just want you to know the whole time we have been doing this I have been on the Facebook page looking at your face. You're gorgeous.

RDY: Oh, thank you!

LM: You have a real... you know, your eyes… you are beautiful!

RDY: Thank you very much.

LM: So, please do write this book. Please, continue to share. I've always had weight issues. Because, I'm an emotional eater. I really have to work at maintaining my weight. Because, you know, traveling, and the food is horrible, and you're getting in at 11 o'clock.

RDY: Oh, yeah.

LM: You get room service, and it sucks. Or, you just eat the bread and butter. Or, you're at the airport for six hours and you're going, "I'm so deprived. I'm eating all the candy in this place!"

Or, you go out and people are going, "Have a drink, have a drink!" And you're going, "Oh, ok. All right. I've had such a sucko day. Sure, I'll have a drink." I just then have to come home and have to diet. I have to exercise.

It's just this continuous awareness that I have to make...

You know, my big motivation is I have so much money in suits I can't get out of that size.

So, I said to Dan the other day, "You know, I've been really dieting the last couple of weeks to get my ass in my suits."

So, I got back to my weight and it means just being very mindful of everything I put in my mouth. Not to eat unconsciously.

RDY: I actually put off writing that book for six months. Because, I said, "How can I write a book on weight loss, if I can't see the fruits of my labor reflected in the mirror?"

I felt like anything that I wrote, I'd feel like a charlatan.

Even though I actually did physically lose the weight. I would still feel like a charlatan. Because, when I looked in the mirror, I still saw fat Rachel.

I mean, I don't anymore. I took six months of really looking hard at myself, truthfully. You know, no one else around, no clothes on.

Ok, this is what I used to look like. This is what I look like now.

Really having to soul search. To find the person that I am *now* versus what I was then.

So, I have just now started rewriting part of it.

LM: Ok. I would like to reframe this new head a little bit.

Can you see yourself as a 'light on earth' who has come to experience this experience that you've had with your weight? So, you can be a messenger to the world of what's possible. Can you see this as your soul's journey, that...

RDY: Meaning, the reason I feel like I'm here in this life?

Not the copywriting. Not any of the other stuff. I mean, although I absolutely love it. Like going to an amusement park love it. But, the thing I feel deep down in my gut. The fire that burns in me that makes me want to get out of bed in the morning is I see so much of this country is just grossly and clinically obese.

Yes. And there are so many things that are just little, bitty, things they can do to extend their life. To give them a better quality of life. To allow them to do so many things with their kids, and with each other. And to be more content in their own skin that it's just little things.

But, it seems so insurmountable when you have got so much weight to lose.

So, I feel like the thing that I'm supposed to do is not to teach people about wealth attraction, or writing the next greatest sales letter.

It's to show people that if you just take little itty bitty steps. Just do this one little thing. Throw out the first bite next time you want to eat.

You can have a Snickers bar if you throw out the first bite. That way you psychologically have not eaten the entire Snickers bar. So, you're not going to deal with the guilt.

You know, just little things like that. If they do a bunch of little things it turns into something big.

I grew up in Japan. And in Japan that's called 'Kaizen'. Where you take little, bitty steps to achieve a huge result. That's what I really feel like I was put on earth to do.

LM: Well, the whole time you talked I've had chills all over my arms!

By the way, that means angels are around me, and that means truth! So, without sounding tough here, the whole copywriting thing, that's just at this moment in time.

What you just said to me is really a million percent more important. Because, the small piece of pie who are going to do copywriting in their life, versus as you said, the epidemic of obesity, and them being roll models for their children, who will be obese is a million times more important.

RDY: You know, I've got eight year old twins. My oldest is 13. One of the twins is very artistic, loves to draw.

The other day they came in with a picture of a teddy bear that had sweat dripping down its face, and had big huge lumps on his arms where the muscles were. And was holding dumbbells, and said, "I drew this for you."

And I said, "That goes on the fridge right now." I have tears streaming down my face. Because it meant that they were watching...

LM: Yes, because what you are and what you do are 10 times more important than anything you say!

RDY: Yes.

LM: You know, the greatest gift you really have on earth is your example. I would love for you to say that in the book when you get that! I believe this with my heart. The greatest thing you can do in life is to give a greatest example.

I mean, to be the living example of you're not perfect. But, that you're taking small steps every day towards a better life and that you are taking responsibility for your own health!

So, you and I are very much on the same page.

I'm very honored that... you know, by the way. I rarely accept these kind of invitations, Rachel.

I mean, I get like 20 of these interview invitations a month. And, you know, I get a feel for the person, and then I go, "Well, nah."

But, when you asked me, I just didn't even hesitate! I just, yes.

And, I was actually surprised at myself, since I had said to myself back in August that I was going to do none of this.

So, I'm very honored to have had this opportunity with you!

RDY: I'm very honored you said 'Yes'! I'll admit. I was pretty surprised that you said "Yes", too!

LM: Well, thank you. And I really will tell you, I *am* a millionaire. I qualify to be in this book.

RDY: Well, just in doing the math on how many people you have in *Peak Performers* and in your monthly calls that you do, I did the math and I said, "Yeah, unless she is just spend crazy."

LM: No, no, no, no. And look. I just bought a lot next door to me and spent a million dollars 2 years ago in cash. I bought an office building a couple of years ago. I live on the beach. I'm debt free. I don't owe anybody a penny on the face of the earth. Not a penny.

I'm a big conservative. I live under my means. I'm not a 'showy', try to impress you with stuff, person. I like to have money in the bank. I like to be debt free. I wasn't kidding when I said I have six years worth in savings of living expenses. Not six months, six years!

If you're a millionaire, you can take an afternoon off. You should have arranged your life, so life is now working for you. You're not working for it!

This is the really interesting thing about life…All of us really know the truth, if we'll just allow it in. Sometimes it's inconvenient. But, when I'm dealing with people…

Like, if I'm hiring someone, Rachel… I don't really give a damn about their resumé.

I hardly look at it. I'm really more interested in what I'm feeling with that person. You know, I'm going to put them through my own little test…

'If you went to such and such college, I don't really care. You learned to memorize a bunch of stuff. Well, good for you. But, what can you do?' I really live my life more from feeling… 'Is this truth?'

I'm totally and 100 percent congruent with what we're putting out. Because if I am not, then I'm out of integrity with myself.

So, with all that said, I'm wishing you millions of dollars of prosperity. How about that?

RDY: Oh, fantastic. Thank you, thank you, thank you.

LM: All right. So, I'm looking forward to the transcript of this interview! Because I always amaze myself when I read stuff I say.

In fact, I read a transcript the other day that I was like, "Wow." I talked about being arrested in Israel as a Spy. And I had forgotten that story for a while. But, that's a fun story.

I used to be a professional photographer. I was traveling all over the world. I had been in Africa. Then I had gone to Egypt for a long time. Then I went to Israel… Well, the authorities in Israel were not happy with my passport. And, when you're gone three months and they asked you where you were three weeks ago. Hell, I don't know where I had lunch yesterday.

I'm a very forward person. I couldn't remember. Then, all hell broke out after that. But, anyway, it's a funny story now! So, life is long. Life is an adventure.

RDY: Lee, thank you so much! I just appreciate it so much!

LM: Thank you.

Jason Oman's comment on Lee Milteer's chapter

One of the great things Lee mentioned is the importance of developing great work ethic. That comes from conditioning your mind and body to consistently take action. Then stay with that task till it's finished. Remember that no matter how daunting the task, there is always a way!

Take responsibility for your own success and wealth by taking the actions required to make it happen.

Also, be sure to celebrate your failures! Because future successes typically come from lessons learned from past failures.

As Lee said, you need to 'Master Yourself'. Be willing to do the work within: work on your self-esteem, your self-image, and your view of your self-worth. Lee also said, "If you really want to be a millionaire, you have to go past what other people think into thinking, there is no one like me in the entire universe. Celebrate that! Don't compare yourself to other people."

Chapter 3:

Kendra Todd – Winner, Season 3 of Donald Trump's Apprentice

Rachel D. Young: First, if you don't mind… We can just kind of get the elephant in the room out of the way. You know, all that to say, yes, let's talk about Donald Trump.

You were the Season 3 Apprentice TV show winner. You were the youngest and the first woman to win the coveted nod from the Donald. But, you were already successful before the Apprentice, right?

Kendra Todd: Yeah, I was. I had a very successful Real Estate career in South Florida.

It really took off with the Real Estate boom, and the ironic thing is, I didn't know what I wanted to be when I grew up. I always thought I would be doing big things and I just couldn't wrap my mind around how to start small and think big!

Like a lot of people's stories. It was just very serendipitous how I got into Real Estate. I never thought of myself as someone who excelled in sales or marketing. I got into Real

Estate because I graduated college during the recession in 2000 and I couldn't get a job.

So, what happens when you can't get a job is you either don't work, or you invent your own job.

So, I headed down that path of being an individual entrepreneur in Real Estate, really for lack of other options. I discovered throughout the process that I was really great at sales and marketing.

I never would have discovered that if I had been closed-minded and said, "Well, I am not good at those things or I am not interested in that." I was really sort of forced to think outside the box, to go outside my comfort zone, and to try an industry in an area that I didn't realize I had natural ability in.

The lesson I learned from that is I think sometimes we put boxes around our idea of what we can do, what we should do, and what we are good at. But, by doing that, we eliminate the possibility of discovering unique talents we didn't realize we have.

Well, I ended up having a really successful Real Estate career because of it.

RDY: So, you were successful doing Real Estate and you were getting ready for the auditions for the Apprentice. Was there ever a time when you were thinking, "This is completely nuts. There's no way they are going to choose me. There's no way I am going to get on the show. I should just go back to what I was doing..."? Were there doubts or second guesses?

KT: You know, I really went down there... I got dragged down there. I'm not a person who would ever say to myself, "Oh, I want to be on TV and let the whole world watch me be filmed." I'm more of a private person than the life I lead, ironically.

Somebody actually talked me into going down there and part of my reason for going down to the auditions was as a recruiting opportunity. Because there were all sorts of young go getters there that I thought would be good to possibly recruit for my own Real Estate business.

So, I kind of rationalized it as a business opportunity and also just kind of a fun experience, too. I'm one of those, 'oh, why not?' kind of people. But, I didn't really think about the outcome too much.

I think my biggest fear was to be sitting at the initial table and saying something silly, or not getting picked. But, I didn't go there to be like, "I have got to get this." I never in a million years thought it would turn into what it did.

RDY: Wow. So the thing that I loved watching, and I promise this is the last Apprentice question, because I really want to get into what happened afterwards, is that you were tenacious. But, you were also very likeable.

Would you say those traits have assisted you in your success as a broker, an author, an entrepreneur? I mean, even before the show. Were you like that as a child? That tenacious about getting what you wanted?

KT: I'll put it this way. Before I was born, my mom thought that I was going to be a boy and she thought I was going to be a linebacker. I think it's simply innate. I think this is just my DNA.

I'm definitely tenacious and assertive because I am passionately driven. I can't bring myself to do something I don't believe in. Because if my heart isn't in it, then I'm just going through the motions and I feel like a fraud.

So, I've had a lot of periods of waiting in my life, where I didn't go down certain paths because I knew it wasn't for me. And I stood still and just sort of waited.

I'm also a faith driven person and I'm a strong Christian. So you have to understand the periods of waiting, from my perspective, are sometimes your greatest periods of growth and change and they don't require movement just for the sake of action.

So, that's my philosophy. But, my tag line for my business and my entire philosophy is: Live your passion. Share your prosperity. I think one of the things that makes women such great entrepreneurs, who reach levels of success that exceed men many times, is because we are innately nurturers.

We're more likely to be driven to do things out of a desire to build up, encourage, nurture, and see other people succeed. That type of momentum is contagious and once you go down that path it's kind of hard to stop.

Authenticity, likeability, approachability, those are are all ingredients that are crucial to a successful business and a successful brand. And I think that women really excel with the care factor.

RDY: Now, it's interesting that you bring up nurturing. Because the one trait I've seen in all the women I've interviewed, and I've talked to some really fantastic women for this book! The one thing that I have noted across the board is the trend of gregariousness. So, I've asked the other ladies and so I want your opinion on this, too... Do you think women can be successful in business and not just be the docile, genteel nurturers we are sometimes raised to be?

KT: Well, sure. I think there are many paths to success. But, I think the question then becomes, 'what is the long-term shelf life based on the approach you take?' And, 'how satisfying is the life that you lead and the career that you have?'

I think those are the real questions. Because, for me, success is less about how far have I climbed, and more about how far reaching is the impact along the way?

RDY: Wow, that's good. So, I don't know if you were aware of this before we got on the call. But, I invested in single family properties in Georgia for several years. So your path to success being in Real Estate was especially interesting to me. So, I'm curious about your answer to this one...

Why Real Estate? I mean, why not department store manager, or fashion designer, or something more girly? When you picture 'marketing' and 'sales' it can be more aggressive than most women feel comfortable being. But yet, I absolutely loved every second of it. So why not something a little more... I don't even know what the word is...

KT: Well, I think for me, to be honest, I didn't know what I wanted to be when I grew up. I kind of fell into Real Estate. Do you know what I mean?

I wasn't a little girl saying, "I want to be the Nation's Top Real Estate Broker!" It wasn't about a fascination with Real Estate. I think for me, it was just more of a serendipitous thing where Real Estate just happens to be the vehicle that fuels the machine called my business.

The other answer to that question is that Real Estate is tangible. It's a necessity. Everyone needs a roof over their head. And it's fun. You get to work with so many different people. I mean there's just so much to love about Real Estate, because everyone has a need for housing!

You know, I really like dealing in markets that have tangible assets and I really like dealing in Real Estate.

I have the opportunity to not only work with other colleagues in the Real Estate industry. But, also regular people. And that's fun and that's satisfying.

For most people, purchasing a home is their largest investment. And, you know, being able to guide them through that process is very satisfying, I think.

And also with the numbers. I like the fact that Real Estate is a great long term investment. I mean, Real Estate is just multi-faceted and there are just so many layers and so many ways to get involved!

And there is a lot of stuff tied into it, too! You have staging, interior design, and all sorts of other things that you can do! But really, what I love about it is, I love the marketing. I do. I love the marketing. I love finding out new ways to successfully market Real Estate. And I love it as an investment!

I have never been a girlie girl. And so some people might just think, 'Why not something more girlie?' But, I've never been a real girlie girl.

You know, I can probably play a pretty successful game of basketball in an evening gown and a pair of high heels!

So, I think it's kind of fun to be both an ultra-feminine woman who can be really assertive in the workforce too. And be a go getter! I think it's so great to be able to be an equal balance of both!

RDY: Oh, yes! Now, you have a new book that just came out called *'Risk and Grow Rich'*. And to be honest with you, the title sounded a lot like it was inspired by Napoleon Hill.

KT: Yeah, one of the best books ever written! It should be number one or number two in everyone's must read list!

RDY: So, was he a major influence on you growing up?

KT: No. But his book had an influence on me. You know, I think mindset has always been something that is really key for me. But, his book definitely had an impact on me. But, not when I was growing up. I had no idea who he was when I was growing up.

RDY: So, who *was* influential in shaping the way that you turned out?

KT: My mother, my father, and God. I would say the people that I admired growing up were Amelia Earhart, partially because my dad is a pilot. He was a fighter pilot, a top gun instructor, and now he's a commercial airline pilot.

So, I wanted to be like my dad when I grew up. So, of course, I gravitated towards aviation.

But, Amelia Earhart did what everyone said a woman couldn't do. And, she succeeded! I just always loved Amelia Earhart and what she represented!
I think when I got older, I really formed a great admiration for Oprah. I have always loved television as a medium to really impact people and inspire them.

I really just love what Oprah brought to the table at the pinnacle of her career. So, I wanted to follow in her footsteps in some fashion. So, I would say those two people really influenced me.

RDY: You know, you can learn something and go forward with the knowledge you've gotten and then you can go back to doing it the way that you used to.

So, as you got into business and you were exposed to more entrepreneurial-minded authors and philosophers, and people like... I'm sure Robert Kiyosaki for example, with Rich Dad Poor Dad?

KT: Actually, that is the reason I got into Real Estate. It was 'Rich Dad, Poor Dad'.

RDY: Really? Me, too!

KT: Yeah, that was the turning point for me. One of my friends just had it on her coffee table and she wasn't really into it and she was kind of like, "Do you want to borrow it?"

So, I burned through it in two days and I sought him out not long after that and actually interviewed him and Kim. And

I've known them ever since. But, I actually met Robert and Kim before the Apprentice.

So, Robert actually told me he turned on the television one day and was like, "Oh, look, it's Kendra!"

RDY: 'Rich Dad, Poor Dad' and Robert Kiyosaki had a tremendous impact and influence on the way I thought about money and business…

KT: And how important it was! And then, of course, Think & Grow Rich is right up there. That's really just more for money mindset.

The reason why I wrote a book called *Risk and Grow Rich* is because I think that first and foremost your mindset is what is most important. And I used to have a tremendous fear of taking risks. And a lot of opportunities passed me by. I mean, I was a fearful creature. And I was afraid to go out and try anything in life if success wasn't certain. And there is no such thing as certain success in life.

So, I literally was just stagnant for years in my life and very unhappy and wasn't going anywhere and I looked in the mirror one day and was like, "What are you doing? What are you waiting for? Why are you such a little scaredy cat?"

And something just changed. I think I just reached the end of myself and I got tired of my 'Poor Me' mentality and my switch just kind of flipped.

So, when I wrote that book, it was really less about Real Estate and more about our relationship to Fear of Failure. And how to mitigate, analyze, mediate, and measure risk so that you can see smart risk and you can distinguish it from bad risk.

So, that it is more of a mathematical equation and you can actually do Risk Analysis which I think is really the way women's minds work anyway. Men tend to jump first, think later. Women tend to do all their research first and sometimes opportunities will pass us by because we over plan, we over prepare, and we over think things.

So, I think that there has got to be that meeting in the middle. It's like the meeting of the Mars and Venus. I think you have to sort of meet somewhere in the middle, for most women in order to have balanced success.

RDY: Now, in talking about success, how do you define it? I mean, is it money? Is it power? Is it prestige? Is it all of the above? How do you know when you've made it?

KT: When I am changing. When I am talking live and someone walks up to me and says, "You inspired me." Or, "something you said", or something they saw you do, or "something you wrote about changed the way I think". And if there has been a positive result because of that. I think that when you put other people's success first, when you make other people's success your priority and your mission, the blessings the Lord gives to you are abundant.

And I think your own success is simply a side bar. You know, I am very sacrificial and selfless in my approach to business. I care about other people. I care about their success.

So, money comes from that. If prestige comes from that, then it is all a gift from God. It is not from me. It is nothing I did. You know, we are not in charge. I mean, I just can't separate my belief system from my fundamental approach to business because it is what drives me.

So, I know success for some people is being a great mother. Success for other women is being successful at work, or being taken seriously by your peers, and for others it's leading a balanced life. Success is defined differently for each person.

RDY: And that is what I wanted the folks who are going to read this to see. The women who will read this to say, "Success is not just a dollar amount."

KT: A dollar amount is a side bar to success. Money is a side bar to success.

RDY: So, I was watching this interview with Gordon Ramsey, the chef, right? And he said that the thing he loves most about everything he does is that no two days are the same. You know, he's got all of these television shows and restaurants and books etc. But, no two days the same and that's why he loves the life he has right now.

And you have got a lot going on, too! You know, you have the spokesperson thing for guard dog and the book. You're an author. You're an investor. You're a philanthropist.

KT: I have a TV show. I'm a Fox News correspondent. I have a Real Estate business. I mean, I do all sorts of things.

RDY: Is there a day coming when you can just rest on your laurels and say, "Whoo. I'm glad all that is over with"? Or, is this something you're doing now because you're loving everything that is going on?

KT: I'm doing it because I love doing it! I'm doing it because I'm letting the Lord guide me. And if he changes all of that one day and puts finality on this and says, "All right, Kendra. Now it's time to be a mom and to be a wife," you know, I would flip the switch and I would go do that. If my calling is to do it all, I will do it all!

So. I'm a forward thinker. But, at the same time, I think it's important to take each day as it comes. I think you have to have both outlooks, both perspectives about the future and about the right now.

But, I do this because I am passionate about people. And as long as I love what I'm doing, and I think that I'm where the Lord has called me to be, then this is what I will do. If he takes me down a path that I don't understand, I will go obediently.

Like I said, I'm guided. I'm guided by my faith. But, I think that as long as I'm helping people and I'm seeing that there is good fruit that comes from the seeds that I'm planting, then I will always be satisfied and happy.

It's what I do with my time. But, I think part of the DNA of an entrepreneur is mixing it up. I think most entrepreneurs are type A personalities, probably all of us. But, we get bored easily.

We like to be creative constantly, challenged creatively. I think that is part of what drives us forward.

So, I bet a lot of the people you're interviewing kind of have their toes dipped in a lot of different ponds.

But, the idea of the challenge, the creative challenge, is to tie all of those different bodies of water together. To take all of those scraps and tie them into one glorious patchwork blanket of a business. Then to take a step back, and see what it is you've created, when you connect all the dots.

But, I think it's important also not to be a spider, too. You have to make sure that all of the different things you're doing are tied together and really do align with the brand. The overall brand you're trying to accomplish.

RDY: Now, here's a question I hadn't planned on asking, but it's just something that popped into my head…You talked a lot about your faith and the way the Lord leads you. And my parents, you probably didn't know this, are missionaries and I grew up in Japan.

KT: I didn't know that!

RDY: I think probably one of the craziest things, at the time, in my father's mind, was back in 1987 when he and my mother felt like the Lord was calling them to completely up root their lives in North Carolina and move both themselves, and my three siblings, over to a country where we didn't speak the language.

We didn't know anything about the culture. We knew nothing. And I was there for seven years. My parents were there for 13.

Is there a calling you've received that has just been so completely 'out there' that you were just like, "Really, God? I mean that seems kind of... That's a little..."

You know, did you ever have that 'Moses and the burning bush' kind of feeling?

KT: I think when Donald Trump said, "You're hired" with 16 million people watching! I was like, "Why me, Lord? Why me?" You know, "What is this? What do you want?" You know, "How do you want to use me?" And, "I hope I don't fail you." For me, that really was my 'Moses moment'.

Because, I'm not the great speaker. Aaron is a great speaker. You know, I don't have words of conviction to persuade. So, I really struggled with that for a couple of years. You know, every day I kind of go, "Lord, why me? Why me?"

And, it really took me awhile to come to a place of total obedience where instead of waiting for the answers, I have started to live the 'whys'. If that makes sense to you.

RDY: Yes, it does. It does completely. I've often thought of my father as the most courageous man I know of to just make that leap. To go all the way around the world and live there. And have his kids riding the train an hour to go to school every day and how completely different our lives have become as a result of it.

So, I'm always interested to hear someone whose faith is as solid as yours. But, there had to be a time, where you were like, "Wait, what? You want me to do what? No."

KT: For me, I'm sure I'll probably have moments like that in the future. But, I tried to get out of Real Estate, because I got burned out. I really had a mega successful career in a short amount of time and I burned myself out.

I got guided right into television right as the Real Estate market was crashing in South Florida.

I always had a desire to do TV, but I never pursued it. That blessing was just placed right in my lap. So, I was doing that for a couple of years, and the whole time I was doing that, instead of paying attention to where God had placed me, I was focusing on 'I want to... I want to do this. Or, I want to do that.'

I was the money expert for the Montel Williams show when that was on the air. And I really loved that. I wanted to pursue that. But, the Lord just kept putting me back in Real Estate and I just was really aggravated.

You know, it's really interesting…Here I have this successful TV show. I've been a frequent Real Estate correspondent for Fox News for almost five years now. They call me all the time. And I wasn't leveraging any of that because I wasn't interested in being a Real Estate guru.

I finally came to a place of obedience where I was like, "Lord, this is where you want me." Because when I moved here to Seattle, Real Estate was the last thing on my mind. But, it's the first door that he opened for me. So, I finally was like, 'ok, I've got to stop fighting his will.'

So, I think that's also something... It might be more faith-based than 'business advice', but where we are called to be is not necessarily where we desire to be.

And we just have to have faith that he has plans that are so much bigger and better and more exciting and more awesome than anything our little minds can conjure.

RDY: So, when Donald said, "You're hired," I mean, that's like pretty sudden fame. Did you have any kind of fear of success?

KT: I never had fear of success. I always had fear of failure.

And now, I don't think twice about doing things. As long as I know that I'm following the Lord's will.

But, I've gone pretty far on my own will. But, I've come to the end of it every time. And that is ultimately not satisfying. So, I don't even question whether or not something is going to be successful if I know that I'm walking in the path that I'm supposed to.

But, if I'm not, I know. Because then I fear. I fear failure and success all at the same time. And that's why I know I'm probably walking a path that isn't the right fit for me.

Wow, this has been a pretty fun conversation!

RDY: We have a lot more in common than I thought we did!

KT: Well, the possibilities are endless! You know, I have never had a real job. Everything I have ever done has been: *I have an idea. Let's do this. Oh, I have another idea. Let's do that!*

And aside from my television work, which just dropped in my lap, I have just always pursued my own dreams and just sort of figured out a way to make them work and it hasn't been pretty.

Getting from point A to point B is not a perfect line. There's a lot of fumbling and failure along the way.

But, the way my life goes and the type of person I am is really just like a true entrepreneur. Where there is an idea that just sort of germinates below the surface and you just water it and see if it sprouts.

If you have an entrepreneurial spirit, I think that is the only way you can live. I mean that is just the way we are structured.

RDY: Yeah, you have piles of paperwork everywhere. Eventually you go through the pile and you whittle it down to where it's manageable. You come back around, and there is another stack of papers! That's just a roller coaster. I wouldn't have it any other way!

KT: Yeah, it is. I collect magnets and I have all these magnets on my fridge and one of them says, "When the roller coaster of life gets a little crazy, just throw up your hands in the air and enjoy the ride!"

RDY: That's it exactly!

KT: Yeah. I'm glad I can tell you I actually DO lead my life this way, because I didn't always. It matters less what you do and more how you go about doing it…

So, I think that's great advice for women, too! You don't have to have the *'million dollar idea'*. Most million dollar ideas are not huge 'Aha moments'. They're just very simple ideas where there's a need and somebody fills it.

They're usually not ground breaking, Nobel Prize winning ideas. They're simple ideas, and simple needs, that people are just not filling properly.

So, it's more about how you go about doing it that will determine your success. And the people you align yourself with along the way.

It's less what it is that you're doing...I mean, that's a radical departure from most philosophies of success. But, I think that's the truest one!

RDY: Thanks so much for taking the time to talk with me today! This has been a lot of fun!

KT: Listen. Have a really wonderful day and when we get off the phone from this, say a prayer that the Lord just really takes this project of yours and he really takes it to reach woman!

RDY: Oh, I would love that so much. Thanks so much!

****Jason Oman Comment on Kendra Todd chapter****

One of the really great things Kendra mentioned was that she discovered 'Natural Talents' she didn't even know she had which helped her create incredible success!

So, it makes sense to spend some time to figure out and discover what YOUR Natural Talents are as well! In fact, ALL of the most successful people I've met & studied went farther in their success as a result of utilizing their Natural Talents!

Kendra also said, "million-dollar ideas are almost never huge and out of your reach." So, this means it's possible for YOU too! You just need to take action to figure out a good idea for a highly-desirable product, service, or information!

Chapter 4:

Ali Brown – INC 500's Fastest Growing Companies

Rachel D. Young: Let's get right to the meat and potatoes, Ali. At this point, you're successfully juggling several different brands.

You've got several different companies, coaching programs, and the several times that I've heard you on stage at various events, you're on vacation more than you're working it seems like! So, I know you've had huge success!

But, before we get into the big success of it all, I want to go back. Because I know at one point you were working in New York. You were earning a living while your boss was getting rich.

I want to know what was the catalyst that made you want to be your own boss? Was there like a deciding moment where you said, "All right, I've had enough"?

Ali Brown: I actually remember. It's funny. I was working at a small Ad Agency at the time, and this is only 10 years ago. At the time, I was a copywriter. I had to work my way up to being a copywriter at the company. But, I was getting very frustrated being told when to be at the office. And that I couldn't come and go. I really wished I could be working at home. And there was this freelance designer who would come and go as he pleased. I noticed that he would do his work in the park, or at home, or he would come back all tan.

I would be like, "Where have you been?" He'd say, "I've been on vacation. But, I brought the work with me." So, I'm thinking, 'That just seems so amazing. I didn't know you could do that. I just didn't know that existed.' So, that's probably when I got that feeling. I was really envious!

You know, when I coach women in my programs, we're taught to think that 'envy is a really bad thing'. And I think it's a good thing when you're aware that it's indicating something that you want in your life, whether it's more money, more success, or for me, it was freedom.

It was really the freedom factor that was a trigger for me wanting to make the leap. And then, the income on top of that was a bonus once I figured out how to run a business.

I was so happy to work in my crappy apartment. I can't tell you. I was delighted just to be in my crappy apartment with my dial-up modem. I was living in the West Village in New York City at that time just to be able to walk around and sit in the coffee shop.

But, I didn't have that *big vision* in the beginning. I didn't see any of this coming! My big vision was to pay my rent working for myself. I mean, for me, that was the end all.

I barely pulled it off that first year. I probably didn't even do that fully until the second year. I was just so happy and my friends thought I was nuts!

My parents, I didn't even tell them for like a month or two that I quit my job. Everyone thinks you're crazy! But, you know in your heart it's the right thing for you. And when I look back, I want to just hug that little girl.

She seems like a little girl to me, and just say, "I'm so proud of you for doing that!" I can't believe she had the courage to do that at the time!

RDY: Now, you bring up an interesting point. Because, I know I read at one point that you couldn't even pull money out of the ATM to go have drinks with your friends. Because, you only had like 18 bucks in the ATM.

AB: $18.56. I will never forget that!

RDY: Wow. At that point, how did you find the will power to keep going? Because, I've been rich and I've been broke. I remember in the broke times, I wanted so badly just to go, 'you know what? This sucks! I hate being broke!' It would be so much easier to just go get a job. What made you keep going on the path that you were on?

AB: I think it was a little bit of stubbornness and a little bit of pride. Honestly, at that point, I had started my business. And everybody knew it. I wanted nothing to do with having to go back and get a job!

I would have lived on the street first. I really just wanted that freedom so badly. I just went day by day. It was scary, and I wasn't quite sure what I was doing all the time. But, I think you just take it one day at a time.

What's interesting is, now I have a multi-million dollar company. This year we're in the Inc 500 list of the fastest growing companies in the nation!

But, those fears don't go away. They're still always there a little bit when you are taking those big leaps.

Or, maybe it's a day that some projects aren't coming together. Or, you're waiting for a check. A big check that doesn't come in. And, you just realize, it's all the same!

You just have to get comfortable with the risk and comfortable with the growth. So, mastering that at a small level and just getting through those days when you don't know what you're going to do. That really sets you up for the larger level. I think first you show the universe you can handle the little things. And then the bigger things start to arrive.

RDY: So, if you were going to look back on everything that you went through and do it all over again… The quitting your job. The struggling to pay your bills. All of it. Is there anything that you would change or do differently?

AB: Well, it's not something I could've done really. But, I wish that I had found a mentor. I wish that I had met someone to kind of take me under their wing. Or, at least show me how to run a business. I had no money, though. I didn't go to seminars at that time. I did get books. I bought some books from the bookstore. I listened to Tony Robbins cassettes. Remember cassettes?

Which is funny, actually, because Tony is interviewing me for an upcoming series. Isn't that amazing? I talked to him and I said, "This is going to sound crazy. But, I need to tell you that I listened to your cassettes on the subway."
I get a little emotional when I think of this. That I had no one to tell me that I was going to be ok. I had no one to say, "You can do this." I had no one to say, "I believe in you."

I mean, I remember having a boyfriend at the time. He just thought I was just out of my rocker trying to do this on my own. But, I just knew that I was meant to do something amazing. I wasn't sure if that was what was it. But, I couldn't do it working for someone else.

I think for many of us, who have become entrepreneurs, it's just so painful to be that bird in a cage at that job. That you are willing to try some crazy things and live on the edge for a while just to figure things out, which is the opposite of how we're programmed to play it safe, and take things one step at a time, and one ladder rung at a time. Instead of take these leaps. And people wonder how I've gotten where I've gotten. And, it's not because I played small. It's because I just went all out!

RDY: I always say that, 'We got here because we're like bumble bees.' The way they're designed, they shouldn't be able to fly. But, nobody ever bothered to tell them that.

AB: You're right. Yeah, aren't they anatomically completely incorrect? Like, basically should not be able to fly.

RDY: Yeah, we didn't know any better. We didn't know that we should be failing at something. So, we just kept going until it worked. I think that's a lot of where that came from.

You know, in listening to you talk, I think back to the other interviews that I've done. And, there's one thing, one common denominator, among all of these successful women that I have talked to, which is, if you were going to pick one word that describes your rise to the top, your ability to be successful…

Are you tenacious, or gregarious? Are you aggressive? Was it just plain smarts? Dumb luck? What would you say got you to where you are now?

AB: Courage. I vacillate between courage and love. Because, I truly believe that just coming to love who I am and being happy with everything: the mistakes, the flops, the failures, the embarrassments. I still have to love that.

I have to love it all. Because, it's me. And I run my business very faith based. I remember that I was created in the image of our creator. Of God. Universe. However you want to think of it.

And, you have to love everything that comes with that. And, as imperfect as a being as you are, you have to love that and bring that to the world. But, that takes courage. So, for me, they go together. The one word goes into two or three words. But, it was those two things. It was courage and love.

RDY: So, were you always like this? Was there something in your childhood that kind of prepped you for this?

AB: I was probably the least likely to ever be an entrepreneur! I cried when I was forced to sell *Girl Scout cookies*. I did. I hid them in the closet! I ate most of them. I did. I tried to eat them. I didn't want to sell anything. Even in High School. You know? Do you remember? Did they make you do those *Fund Raisers*? Like sell the candy and stuff? I would just ask my mom, "Please, can we just buy this or give it to friends or something?" I just could not stand it. And my father had a business with his father. But, all I saw growing up was his being gone all the time.

When he would come home, he would be in a horrible mood. And he just really kind of wanted to be alone.

So, all I heard about having a business was: stress, and how he always didn't have the money to pay his employees, and things were up and down, and it eventually killed him. I'm very happy that we developed a strong relationship in the last years before he died.

But, you know, while growing up I didn't know anything about running a business, or being an entrepreneur. What I did see was my dad was more stressed than my friends' dads who had corporate jobs, would come home at five, and be there for dinner. So, I didn't really have a good model of what being an entrepreneur really could be like. That's why, what I live, and what I teach is so critical!

Setting your business up around how you want your life to be, and not the opposite. Many of us fit into rolls, and businesses, or companies that we adjust our lifestyle to. I want you to start with the Lifestyle that you want and design your business around that.

When my dad was really sick in the end, I was so grateful and felt so blessed that I could hop on a plane in two hours and fly to Texas where they were at the time and be there for him.

I remember when I was walking into the ICU, he was happy to see me. But, the first thing he said was, "What about your business?" He was worried that I was there.

I said, "Dad, I brought my business with me. I pointed to my laptop." We take for granted that that's possible now. That we can set up a business that is fun. That matches who we are and that we can work from home, or work anywhere. I just think people are crazy if they're not taking advantage of the capabilities to do this now!

RDY: So, to the woman who may be nervous about leading anyone in a company…You know, even if it's just herself in the beginning. What would you say to her?

AB: All you have to do is believe in yourself. And that makes you a good leader! So, don't worry about saying the right things to your employees, or your team, or even yourself. Just know that you have to believe in your decision!

So, whether it is, for example, taking a leap that you intuitively know is the right time for you to do something. Maybe you can't rationalize it. But, you intuitively know you have to believe in yourself. And that takes some practice to get used to. But, I share with everybody that most of the decisions I make are not based on rational facts in my business. It is most often intuition.

I had the pleasure last year of meeting and spending some time with Richard Branson. Who is, I think, one of the most amazing entrepreneurs on the planet. He was sharing with us that, because of his dyslexia actually, he said it really helped sharpen his intuition. Because that's how he made most of his business decisions.

He couldn't read contracts quickly. He couldn't read through paper work, or get all the facts on things.

And, when you look at most business leaders, they really operate just off of their intuition. So, women need to get better at trusting themselves. They try to get all of this outside authority, and information, and it's almost as if they are waiting for permission from someone else to be successful.

If they need that... if you're reading this right now... I am giving you permission to do this.

Because, more women need to step up in their businesses and the world. Because. this is what is going to shift the world and get us back to a place of sanity.

RDY: It's funny that you bring that up. Because another common theme that I'm hearing...One of the staple questions I keep asking is: Do you think women can be born into leadership? Or, is it something that they have to force on themselves in order to lead others? It sounds like you're saying, "Yeah, go with your gut." They call it woman's intuition for a reason!

AB: I do think some people naturally may have leadership qualities. I'll admit, I'm a Leo. So, we're known to be leaders. But, remember that, being a leader doesn't mean that you have to be forceful or dominant. I mean, being a leader is just putting yourself out there, and allowing your message to be heard. And helping others. I mean, there's so much more to leadership than taking over teams, or people, or companies. It's really about just stepping forward in your highest good. That naturally makes you a leader!

RDY: Now, I heard from a lot of the women I've talked to, in preparation for this book, that they were fearful of being their own boss.

Because, if they're a mom, they have mommy guilt. Because, they're busy working on their business, and not paying attention to their kids. Or, they have spousal guilt, where they feel like they're neglecting their spouse. Or, they feel like that they have this finite amount of time. And it has to be spent on either their life or their business. And whichever they devote their attention to, they feel guilty for not focusing on the other.

Do you feel like you missed out on a lot of life when you were struggling to get where you are now?

AB: Yes and no. I mean, I did kind of a different track from a lot of my friends. A lot of my friends seemed to meet the right guy early. Got married. And did the house, and kids, and SUV thing, you know?

I was in New York and I really love the city. I love the energy. And I always felt like I just had to be exploring a lot of things. I was very curious about life and wasn't ready to make a choice yet. And looking back I think everything was just perfect.

I don't regret any of those years of the struggling and figuring out who I was. Because I have such a solid foundation today of who I am. I am so clear of who I am and what I am here to do and how I can help people.

That wouldn't have been possible if I hadn't had to break through those layers of self realization.

I mean, I tell my students, "There is no better personal development tool than starting your own business." This brings up all your bullshit. It really does.

Because you have to be strong. You have to step out there and believe in yourself. And that is more than most people do in a lifetime. You have to get over all your issues, all your childhood stuff. I wouldn't have traded it for the world because it's made me stronger. It starts peeling away the layers of the onion. You get to the core of who you really are.

What's ironic now too, in my life and relationships is; I am finally… I have kind of proven everything to myself that I have had to prove and you know, built this amazing business. And now, I just finally met the right guy.

So, it's taken a while. But, I knew that I had to become who I was supposed to become before some other things happened. So, I did things in a different order. But, I think everyone has a path that they're here to follow, and it doesn't have to look like everyone else's.

RDY: So, I have to ask…When I was getting started, I had to have everything done yesterday. It had to be perfect before I could sell 1. I had to have the entire thing done… You know, the up-sells, the down-sells. All things had to be finished. It all had to be great before I could put it out on the market and see what happens.

When you were developing, you know, I know you've got the jewelry line and you have the magazine. There is the list a mile long, of all the things that you're working on like right this minute… When you were developing all of that, did you struggle with that theme 'Perfection'? That it all has to be just right?

AB: I still deal with that. I have learned to let that go a lot. One thing I learned early on is that 'Good, is good enough.' We all have this perfect vision of how things are supposed to be. And women especially, will procrastinate launching a product, or program, or service. Because they're waiting to get all their ducks in a row, and make sure it is the right colors, and things like that.

I think your offering should be attractive. And all of the basic things you're promising should be in there. But, it doesn't need to be perfect.

And I see a lot of women missing out on things. Because they're taking so long to launch their products and programs. I tell them, "I have never had all my ducks in a row for anything I have ever done!" Some of my ducks are on vacation. They have never been here. I mean, we launch things. We do what we have to do. And then we figure it out as we go. A lot of people see what I do, and they think we must have these like intense strategy meetings, and plan out every detail. But, no. It's just that we're good at moving quickly, and we decide what's important, and get the important things done, and then fill in the blanks as we go. I think that's true when you dig behind the curtain of every company.

It's the ones who don't do that, that I would actually be suspicious of how successful they are. Because, money likes speed. You don't want to be reckless. But, you have to keep in motion. Otherwise you will stagnate.

RDY: I think that is it exactly. I mean, I myself procrastinated for six months. I just launched a new book called *What If You Were Thin?* And, I didn't want to launch it. Because I wasn't at my exact perfect goal weight. I was worried that people aren't going to want to read it if I still have another five pounds to lose.

My husband was like, "You can only throw spaghetti at the wall for so long before you have got to have spaghetti. You just need to serve the meal and be done."

So, I still suffer from just wanting it to be so great, and wanting to help people so badly, that sometimes I let it hinder myself. So, it's nice to hear that I'm not alone.

AB: Yeah, definitely.

RDY: So, now that you've arrived, and you're super successful, and you have so much on your plate that it probably seems like a buffet sometimes. How do you tap it? What is next?

AB: I think this year for me has been kind of making all my dreams come true with the magazine, the Millionaire Protégé Club (which is my coaching company) being able to work with women and mentor them personally. Actually with two of them breaking a million dollars this year, which is very exciting. The boutique, as you mentioned... I am just having so much fun.

I think what happens from here is, my next level of getting really clear on my biggest joys, and focusing on those. I will tell you that it will continue to include live events like my upcoming event called "Shine: Discover your true wealth". I love live events! I'd like to do more of them around the world actually. And also more television. I am really liking TV!

I was actually just on 'E' the other morning! That was my first National Appearance. I really would like a show devoted to woman entrepreneurs. But, not all business. It's business. It's style. It's life just like *Ali* magazine.

I just love what I do and I just want to continue to get the message out around the world that women who work for themselves, I think have the best life! I just see no better way to create an extraordinary life than being an entrepreneur.

RDY: Fantastic! Wow! Thank you so much again, for taking the time to talk with me today! It has reiterated some things that I really wanted to make sure got into the book.But, at the same time, it's even some things that I hadn't even expected...

AB: Oh, good. I'm so glad! Thanks for having me!

Jason Oman's comment on Ali Brown's chapter

As Ali recommended, if you don't have a good role model in your life, you should find one ASAP!

As you develop an 'entrepreneurial mindset', don't try to fit into a pre-existing business model and adjust your life to it. Instead, start with the lifestyle you want and design your business around that.

Ali said 'the best personal development is to start your own business because it makes you face everything about yourself.' I agree with this!

Don't wait until you "Get your ducks in a row before you do anything". Like Ali, I've learned that's not always necessary. Get yourself out there and then adjust as needed. Don't procrastinate just to get everything perfect before you start taking action!

Chapter: 5

Alexis Martin Neely, the Lawyer You Love™

Rachel D. Young: Well, first of all, I know that you're a very busy woman. You've been on television and radio. You've been interviewed right and left. So, let me just say thank you for taking time out of your extremely busy schedule to talk to me today!

Alexis Martin Neely: Oh, well, thank you for including me in this project. It sounds great!

RDY: Now, before we get started on where you are now…Because, it's fun to look at the success of it all, do you mind if we kind of go back in time a little bit? I mean, you know, you spent the past five years doing more than most women think that they can do in a lifetime!

AMN: And it feels a little bit like that. That's for sure!

I guess the best time to go back to is really the time when I was working at a big law firm. I had graduated from law school, and did what I thought I was supposed to do which was to get a job at the best place I could. Which was a law firm called *Mungers, Hole, & Olsen*, started by Charlie Munger, who is Warren Buffet's right hand guy. I started there, and thought I should spend the rest of my career there!

But, after a short while, probably within the first year, I realized that there's a big problem. Because, I was really unhappy at this big law firm.

Here I was maybe 26, 27 years old, and I had done everything I was supposed to do. I had gone to law school. I graduated first in my class. I had clerked for a judge. I got a job at one of the premier law firms in the country. I got married. I had a baby.

And I was miserable. And really felt like my life was not my own. Like, I was *not* in control of my life!

And things started to shift for me, pretty dramatically, when I realized that that wasn't the truth. The truth was that, I was in control of my life, and I had no idea what that meant. But, I could start right where I was!

So, I started at that law firm by saying, "Ok, well, I need..." You know, I was collecting a six figure paycheck, and I'm the bread winner in my family. I have a baby at home and a stay at home husband taking care of the baby.

So, I'm not about to leave the law firm or, at least, I didn't see how that would be possible.So, I decided to make a go of it there and try to build my own practice there.

And the firm was nice enough to allow me to try and bring in clients. And they were very accommodating of that. So, I started to try and do that. I started to really focus in on, 'Ok, how can I take control of whatever I do have control of?' Which was just myself. And what I do on a daily basis to some degree.

So, I started networking and going out and meeting people with the intention of building myself a little Estate Planning Practice while still doing the work of the Law Firm. You know, the work that the lawyers would give me, which made me very unhappy...

The reason it made me unhappy, is because I went to Law School to make a difference! And to have a relationship with clients and to feel like I was bringing people empowerment. And that I was going to be their advocate.

But, that just wasn't what it was about at all! It was about creating some form documents for them. And giving them what I thought of as a sense of 'False Security', thinking that everything had been taken care of. When I knew that it truly hadn't.

Because, when they really needed the documents I was creating, they were going to be out of date, or they weren't going to have been handled the right way to make sure that they worked when somebody needed them. But, I didn't know what to do about that at that time.

I was really stuck doing things the traditional way. It was the only way that I knew. And it was the way I was being trained.

So, then one day, I went to hear a woman speak at a women's networking event. And this was with the local chamber of commerce in my community. And this woman was speaking on Branding.

But, I didn't hear her talking about branding. What I heard her talking about was how much she loved her life! She worked from home. She had her own business. Her child was able to come in and out of her office at any time. She loved her clients and she loved her life!

And a light bulb went off over my head! Oh, I can actually have that kind of a life?

It opened up a whole new possibility for me that I actually didn't have to do things the way I thought I had to do things. The straight and narrow path of College, Law School, go to work for a big firm, work for someone else for the rest of your career. And then, you know, that's the end of that. That maybe I could actually do something different.

But, I didn't know what that meant. I just knew that there was hope! There was possibility! So, I bought this gal's book, not because I cared, as I said, about branding at that point. But, because I wanted to know her secrets to life! How did she have this life that she loved? And how could I create the same thing for myself?

So, I was reading the Acknowledgements of the book, and she was writing about a coach that she worked with. This was 10 or 12 years ago…

And today coaching is totally mainstream! Everybody gets it! But, back then it was weird…And I already felt weird, you know?

I already felt like I didn't fit in. And thinking about the coaching, I was like, 'Oh, I don't know, you know, I never spend money on myself.' So, the idea of spending money to have someone coach me…

You know, I had gone to law school and graduated first in my class. So, I thought I was really smart. And it was very difficult for me to get over this barrier of thinking that I'm going to hire some person who's never been to Law School who's going to be able to help me make smart decisions in a career in law.

So, there was a lot of ego that I had to get over there. Fortunately I did, because I said to myself, "All right, Alexis. You might be smart, but you're really miserable. And here's this woman that you just heard talk who might not be as smart as you, but she is really happy!

So, do you want to be smart, or do you want to be happy?" Well, I decided I wanted to be happy!

So, I called the coach, and I hired her. Which was a huge step for me! I had to overcome skepticism. I had to overcome financial fear. Because even though I was making six figures, we were spending all of it. We weren't keeping any money! Most of it was going to taxes, health insurance, and then, of course, the cost of the baby. And we bought a house, and I never spent any money on myself.

So, this was a big deal!

I started working with this gal, and the first thing she starts doing is talking to me about things like getting my nails done, and getting my hair done, and going to the dentist.

And I was really annoyed. Because, I didn't hire her to talk to me about getting my nails done and getting my hair done!

I told her to talk to me about my work and my business…

And, you know, I *never* got my nails done! I don't think I had ever got a pedicure up to that time, except for my wedding day! And here she is, telling me that these are the things I have go do. And I was really pissed! Then, I said to her, "Why are we talking about this? I want to talk about my business. I want to talk about my work."

And she said, "You're never going to be happy, no matter what you're doing in business and in work, if you're not taking care of yourself!" And that was like a big eye opener! I mean, it seems pretty simple now.

But, back then I never took care of myself! I was too busy taking care of everybody else and I thought that was the way it was supposed to be.

So, little by little, I did. I started doing the things that I needed to do to take care of myself: Dentist, pedicure, working out, doing a little exercise. And it was hard to spend the money on myself, to take the time for myself.

Because here I was away from my kids 12 hours a day, as it was. And, now I'm going to take more time not to go to work and make money… But to, you know, pamper myself? But, I did it. And a big shift started to happen as soon as I did!

One of the things that happened, that was the most transformational was, I was getting up early in the morning to drive into work before traffic. And I would go down town, and work out, and do some exercise in the morning.

So, it was about six in the morning, and I'm driving on the freeway. I have my little black Volkswagen GTI that I'm driving. And it's a beautiful time of day actually, because in L.A. normally there's tons of traffic. But, there's *no* traffic! The sun is just coming up, and there was a car right in front of me, and I'm driving on the freeway. And going a regular speed, and all of the sudden this car in front of me swerves!

And right in front of me, where this car had been, was a huge roll of carpet in the middle of the freeway! So, I had two choices about what to do. I could hit the carpet head on in my little car, or I could swerve and try to go around it. So, in my head, I heard this voice that says, "Turn! Swerve!"

So, I pull my steering wheel to the right *hard*, and all of the sudden, I'm spinning across the freeway. And I hear this other voice in my head. And it says, "Turn into the spin! Turn into the spin!" So, I turned my wheel into the spin, and all of the sudden I come to a screeching halt facing the wrong way on the freeway up against the median!

I get out of my car. I'm shaking, you know, to see, 'Oh, my! What happened? What damage has been done?" And, all of the sudden, I hear another voice in my head. It says "Get back in the car and move now!"

So, I get back in the car, and I move, and all of the sudden exactly where I had been standing just seconds before, another car comes spinning across the freeway and slams head first into the median that I was standing next to! Right where I had been standing! And it was a *huge* wake up call for me! Because, first of all, I could have died in that moment.

But, more importantly, what has happened is, for the first time in my life, I recognized that there was this voice inside of me. This still small voice that I now am *very* intimate with that has always been there. Had always been trying to take care of me. But, I had never been listening to it before!

I realized that for the first time that day, it was always speaking to me in my best interests. It was always trying to help me…

And when I started exercising self-care, doing those little things that this coach first talked to me about that I was so resistant to do, the voice started feeling hurt.

That part of me that was ignored for so long started feeling hurt. So, it could stop harassing me with negative talk. You know, like the little child who's being ignored. And it goes from, you know, "Mommy, mommy, look at me!" To exhibiting really bad behavior to get your attention. And that internal voice is the same.

When you ignore it for long enough, it just starts exhibiting negative behavior. And it starts telling you all of the things that are wrong with you.

It says, "What is wrong with you? Why can't you fit in? How could you be so stupid?" You know, "Anybody else would be grateful to have this job, but not you?" "Oh, no..." You know, all the negative talk that it gives you...

And, I realized that there was another part of it, that if I started listening, and I started paying attention in the form of self care, in the form of getting quiet (although I didn't know that part for quite a long time after that.) But, in the form of paying attention to myself that that voice inside of me actually had all my answers.

So, that day was the first time that I ever really connected with the positive aspects of that voice. The part of that voice, the part of me that wanted my highest good was not all about telling me what an idiot. How stupid I was. You know, all the things that were wrong with me. It was actually here to help me!

And, as a result of that experience... within a year I had decided that I wasn't going to be able to ever be happy working for someone else. And I decided to **leave** the 6-figure paycheck. The big law firm, and start my own firm and that was in 2003.

Then, I gave birth to my son, my second child, in March. And, in August of that year, I launched my own law firm, and I didn't know anything about business! I didn't know anything about what I was doing!

In fact, when I went to give my resignation, this was in July, to the partner at the law firm that I was working for, he said to me, "Don't do it, Alexis. You're not ready. You need a few more years here."

And I said, "No, Steve. I'm going to do it! I'm ready. And thank you so much for all of your guidance. And I'm going to start my own law firm…" And I did! And that was in 2003, August of 2003.

RDY: So, let me ask you this…Because you bring up a great point. It's something that I have harped on with some of my own clients. You talk about feeling bad. Because, now not only were you not being able to spend time with your family.

But, now someone is saying 'Spend the same amount of time away from your family. But, now do it with something that spends money and is self-indulgent rather than on your kids'. And a lot of that, I call it 'Mommy Guilt'.

AMN: Oh, yeah. I had major, major Mommy Guilt! That is for sure!

RDY: How in the world did you overcome that, and deal with it. And say, "You know what? I do need to do this stuff! Because, if I don't take care of me, no one else will?" How did you overcome mommy guilt? Because that's huge!

AMN: Yeah, so, the way that I overcame it in the beginning was one very small thing at a time. So, it started with the exercise. It started with leaving my house in the morning 30 minutes earlier which meant that I missed traffic. So, I could work out before my work day started. And what I said to myself is, "Well, it's ok. Because, she's sleeping anyway."

So, now it's not actually anymore time away from her. And yes, it costs me a little bit of money. But, it's going to be worth it. Because I have to try and do something! I have to do something different…What I'm doing isn't working. I feel terrible about myself. I feel terrible about what I am doing…So, I can take the two or three days a week to leave my house a little bit early and work out in the morning.

And thank God that I did. That I was willing to take one small step. Because, that *one* small step led to everything else!

But, it has to start with that one thing! That one thing that I was willing to commit to, that you're willing to commit to. And say, "Yes! I *am* willing to do this for myself!"

And back then, my awareness was so limited. But, I could do just that one thing.

And what that one thing ultimately led to, is a connection to myself. This connection to the truth. Who I am, which I didn't know what it was at the time. But, that's now what I know it is.

It led to me ultimately building a relationship with God, and that was huge obviously. I mean, that changed my life completely and totally!

It ultimately led to every other thing that has happened in my life! So, if anybody is reading this, and is in a place of not being able to overcome that mommy guilt, just do one small thing! If they just do it, do the one small thing, and see what happens. You don't even have to take my word for it. Don't believe me.

Just try *one* small thing that you commit to doing for yourself, every week, knowing that when you take care of yourself, you are setting an example for your children as to what it means to take care of themselves!

See, the problem is, we were never taught this! We were never... our parents didn't model this for us, how to take care of ourselves in a way that is truly nurturing, not just ourselves, but to our whole family. And it's the best thing that you can possibly do is to take care of yourself first!

RDY: So, you are handing in your resignation. And I went through something kind of similar. But, it was not on as grand of a pay scale as yours.

I mean, for me, it was petrifying to walk away from six figures. And do something that you have no idea how to do! I mean, other than the voice in your head that said, 'Yeah, go for it', that you were listening to, did you have any kind of plan? Or, did you just jump in with both feet and say, "Sink or swim, I'm going to do this"?

AMN: Yeah, the first thing I did is, I started interviewing other women who had done it. Because, the biggest barrier was I had no idea how to do this and I don't even think it's possible! So, I couldn't necessarily overcome the 'How'. And that's one of the things that we really have to let go of as beings. We often times get paralyzed by the 'How'.

But, the 'How' will show up when you're ready, when you make the commitment to do something. You actually don't have to worry so much about the 'How'. That's going to show up. But, what you *do* have to worry about is your *Belief*! So, that was the very first thing that I had to be able to shift, is my belief about this being possible.

And, I remember sitting at home, wracking my brain, and saying things like, "I know men do it. Men start their own businesses. How do they do it? How do they do this? How do they lead? How do they support their families?"

So, instead of talking to men who had done it, I started calling and talking to other women who had done it. I called up women that I knew who had started their own businesses, particularly law firms, and said, "Hey, can I come in and talk with you? Can I come in and meet with you?" And they said, "Yes!"

I didn't only meet with women. I also met with men. Most people were really accommodating. They said, "Sure, absolutely. I would love to... I would love to have you come in and talk with me." So, I did that!

I talked with a friend of mine, Deidre. And, I went to her house where she had started her own law firm. And a friend, Jennifer, she had her own law firm. And this guy, Phil. And this woman, Stacey. And then I began to see. 'Oh ok, if they can do it. I can do it!' I didn't know 'how' still. But, I had the belief. If they can do it, I can do it. So, I started to give myself proof of the possibility. If they can do it, I can do it! And that is a *huge* barrier to overcome!

So, whatever it is that you're wanting to do, start talking to other people that are doing it! Look for other people that are doing it. And let them be the model for you. That is exactly what I did!

So, the key is... if there's anything that you're wanting to do, and you don't believe you can do it, start talking to other people who have done it. Start looking at them. Start seeing. And trust that once you make the commitment to it, and you believe that it's possible, the *how* is going to show up! So, that's what I did. I made the commitment.

I *believed* that it was possible. And, I decided that July 19th was going to be the day that I put in my resignation. Then August 1st, 2003 was going to be the day that I opened the doors of my law firm.

I knew that there were some things that I needed to do before that... Like, I needed to get office space, and I knew that I couldn't afford office space alone.

So, I said, "Well, what's the best way for me to do this where I can go as little *out of pocket* as possible?" So, I found a lawyer in my community who had an extra office that I could move into and who would be willing for me to do some of his work in exchange for rent.

So, I could do 20 hours a month of work on his cases, and not pay rent. That was big! Because, now, at least I didn't have to worry about coming up with all of the costs of the office! All I had to do was get furniture, and a computer which I could get everything used. And then also, there would be people in the office with me, which was really nice. And, it turned out, that was a huge blessing, because I got to see exactly how I *didn't want* to practice law.

Because every evening, if I was ever there late, or if I ever came in on a weekend, or anything like that, I would see these lawyers. They are there are *all* the time. And it's not because the law firm management is making them do it. They *are* the law firm management!

It was because they didn't have any systems, or processes. So, they were constantly scrambling to reinvent the wheel. And I said, "This is not how I want to do this? I want to do it totally different."

So, I had hired this coach, this lawyer-type Business Coach who had been in the field of law for a long time. He was in the field of Business Law for a long time, and he was telling me that I could not do things the way I wanted to do them. I had to do them the old 'traditional' way. I couldn't do things in this new-fangled way that I wanted to do them. I would fail, he said. And especially if I tried to do it without him. Well, I ended up firing that coach!

And, while it's true that I knew nothing about business, within 3 years of opening the doors to my law firm, I was bringing in a million dollars a year of revenue into my law firm!

I completely revolutionized the business model, the way that law was practiced, and implemented a brand new business model that I created that clients loved!

They loved me. They loved my firm. And they were happy to pay our fees, even though we were probably the most expensive in town for what we did. And it worked, because I didn't do what everybody else was doing.

I decided to do something completely and totally different! Driven completely by my vision of what was possible. Not what I had seen already done! And it was really interesting. Because, this lawyer that I moved in to share office space with in August of 2003, within about six months we started talking about what our future together would be. How we would work together on a going forward basis.

And, you know, he's been in practice for 25 years, and he had all these client files. Ideally, he thought, we would partner together and I would take over his practice. I remember saying to him. (His name was Ron.) I remember saying, "Ron, here's what I want. I want an office that is completely different. I want it to be like in a little cottage where people don't have to drive into a parking garage. They don't have to come up 12 floors in some corporate office.

But, instead, where they walk in, and they feel like they're coming into my home. And it feels like we're sitting down together at my kitchen table, and I'm doing their planning for them." I was doing that, estate planning and business planning. And helping them with their family, and with their business, and it was very warm and inviting.

And he said, "Oh! That will never work." There was a property in my town that I had always talked about wanting to have as the location for my practice.

Like, 'Oh, if I could just be in this place. That would be perfect!' And the next day my husband called and said, "There's something happening at that property that you always talked about…"

This was the next day after having that conversation with the lawyer who said it would never work. And you have to be ready for these opportunities. So, I immediately called to find out what was going on with that property. I didn't have any financial resources. I couldn't buy the property.

Again, it didn't happen… there's nothing logical here, nothing rational here, other than I know I'm supposed to be in that property.

So, I call the guy up. As it turns out, it had been purchased by a financial advisor who was going to completely renovate the property. I said, "Well, I hope you're renting space on the property. Because, I'm supposed to have my practice there." And he said, "Well, I'm not. But, keep in touch."

And I did. I continued to call him periodically and say, "How's it going?" And then one day in… this must have been May/June time frame, he called me and said, "Ok, we're done with the renovation and there is space on the property. There's a garage on the property and if you want to renovate it you can move in."

It was one of the back cottages that was a garage. So, I said, "Ok. Let's do it." Again, I didn't have the resources for this. And, yet, the resources showed up. Because, I said, "Yes. I'm going to do this!"

And within two months I renovated this little 500 square foot garage into the most beautiful office ever!

And I have like no design capacity. I have no 'eye' for that sort of thing. And yet, it all came together literally like magic in many respects.

Then, in August of 2004, just one year later, we moved into the most beautiful office space that you could ever imagine! I then built my law firm there for the next four years. Yeah, four years! That's where we revolutionized the business model, and built a million-dollar business!

In 2006, that was the first year I had a million dollars in revenue! That was also the year I decided to start teaching other lawyers how to do what I did in my business.

RDY: Now, the recurrent theme that I'm hearing through your story, which is amazing, is that it doesn't sound like you ever had that *Deer In The Headlights* feeling. I mean, that you ever allowed yourself to be paralyzed by the 'What ifs'.

I think that's the *one* thing that keeps a lot of women from going and starting their own business. I think that's the thing that keeps them from doing it is that *Fear of Failing*. Were you ever tempted to just go back and say, "You know what? This is way too hard! It's harder than I thought. I just need to go back and get a job."

AMN: No, not at that point. Never at any point, while I had my Law Firm, was I ever tempted to do that. But, those points *have* come since then, as I've made more transitions.

So, in 2005, I moved out from my husband, and here I am building this law firm. And moving out, you know, getting a divorce from my husband, and it was an ugly divorce...

I do remember some points, during the divorce itself, where there *were* some thoughts about that, like, "Oh, I'm just going to close down my Law Firm, and make no money, so my husband can't claim that I owe him money. Or, that I have to pay him child support and alimony."

That was a big turning point for me, in terms of being able to step forward and say "No". Because, there were a lot of people that said, "Oh, well, just make it so it seems like you don't make any money." Or, "Make it so it seems like your Law Firm isn't worth anything." But, I decided to do something diametrically opposed to that.

In fact, I said, "No, you know what? I'm going to say, Yes." I'm going to ask, "What does he need in order to feel comfortable financially? In order to make this split OK." And I said 'Yes' to that. And that's when my firm turned into a million dollar Law Firm.

And that's why I feel a lot of people make big mistakes, especially when they're in conflict situations. They shrink themselves in the midst of conflict. Because conflict is hard. And it's scary and it makes us small. But, the opportunity is to make yourself big!

It's to say, "Who do I want to be in the face of this, in the midst of this? Who am I now?" Because I really see every opportunity as an opportunity to be more of who you are! You have to identify, 'who do I want to be?'

'How do I want to be?' And when you step into the truth of that, you grow, and you are rewarded. And so I grew, and I was rewarded! It doesn't mean things were easy. They weren't.

They were really hard actually. They were *really* hard. But, I kept saying 'Yes'.

Even during the times when I was crying and scared, I kept saying, "Yes! I'm going to keep going forward. I'm going to keep going forward!"

So then, fast forward to 2006...

I decided I wanted to take things to another level. I wanted to start training other people instead of just doing everything myself in my Law Firm.

I knew, as I was building my Law Firm, that it was just a weigh station. That I wasn't going to be in my Law Firm forever. Because, it just didn't feel... it's not that it didn't feel big enough. That's not that the right wording...

The impact I was making wasn't big enough! I was serving clients 1-on-1. But, I could never serve enough clients, on a 1-on-1 basis, to make the impact that I felt I was here to make.

And yet, in 2006, I was making a huge amount of money in my Law Firm! You know, a million bucks! But, I was spending *all* of it!

I was spending all of it on figuring out how to make this money in my Law Firm. Because, remember, I didn't have anybody to show me the way.

I was reinventing the wheel. I was learning from a lot of different types of entrepreneurs. Then, taking my learning and applying it to my Law Firm.

And I was making a lot of mistakes and spending huge amounts of money on making big mistakes.

So, it was August of that year…

I was starting to go into my line of credit and that was scary! Fortunately I had a line of credit, because I was running out of cash. I was having cash flow issues.

So, I had been studying Dan Kennedy for about 18 months before that. And studying everything there was about Direct Marketing, all the things that he teaches. And, I was trying it. But, it wasn't working the way I felt like it should be working.

It was *herky-jerky*.
It was painful.
It wasn't easy by any means.
It was really hard!

Oh, and I created my first product, to expand my reach, called, *"My Kid's Protection Plan."* I spent about $15,000 to create this product, and I was selling them like one here and there for $397. The first one I sold was super exciting!

But, after that, it was like, *ok, now what?* You know, how am I going to recover my investment? And I was marketing it all wrong. So, I decided that instead of continuing to learn from books and tapes, I was going to have to go the source. And I went to his last ever *Renegade Millionaire Retreat*.

This was in August of 2006. I flew to Cleveland. I was away from my kids, and already into my line of credit. And now, I was putting *more* money on my line of credit!

I had recently hired some coaches who told me that they could help me do this. But, I left every call with them more confused than I had been, before I got on the call. And, I spent a lot of money with them! So, I was really freaking out!

But, I got on that plane. And I remember getting on the plane saying, "God, I trust that the resources I need are here. I'm going to stay open, and do my part to connect with those resources."

So, I got to the conference. And I stayed open. And I talked to everybody I possibly could! About half way through it, I was feeling a little disappointed. Because, it's like, 'Ok, I'm not learning anything new here. This is all the same stuff I've heard in books and tapes! What am I going to do?' And, all of a sudden, it hit me! I got it!...

Every single person here, who is successful, is in one of Dan or Bill's *Mastermind Programs*. I need to get into one of their programs! So, at the break, I go up to Bill, and I was kind of nervous to do this. But, I went and did it anyway. I said, "Alright, Bill. I need to join your coaching program. I'm so close. I'm right there. I have all these things. And I know that I'm right there! But, I just need some help over the line."

And he said, "You can't. It's totally full!"

So, I was about to ask him if I could hire him for consulting, because I had more money on my line of credit. And he said, "You can't even hire me for 1-on-1. You can't even throw money at this problem. I'm totally full!" And I was very discouraged!

And that voice in my head said, again… "Just ask him if he has any other ideas." But, I didn't want to! I just wanted to turn around and slink back to my table. But, I didn't do that.

I said, "Well, do you have any other ideas for me?"

He looked around the room, and he pointed me to a guy who was standing nearby. He said, "Well, go talk to him."

The guy he pointed me to was a long-time student of Dan Kennedy's. A guy named Dave Dee. I ended up talking with him, and telling him what I wanted to do. I remember him asking me, "Well, how much money do you want to make?"

I said, "I want to make an additional $10,000 a month." Because for me, $10,000 a month, was freedom!

It was my child support, alimony, and the rent on my place. So, if I was making an additional $10,000 a month, I decided I didn't want to see clients. I couldn't see clients.

And he said, "Piece of cake!" And he had already done what I wanted to do! He had been a magician. He went from being a magician doing a whole bunch of shows. You know, 30, 40 shows a month, *which was insane*. To teaching other magicians how to book shows.

So, when I got back home, he sent me a proposal for working together. Some options for us to work together.

And I hired him at $30,000 dollars! This was more than I had ever spent to work with a consultant, or a coach! But, I figured if I would be making $10,000 a month after working with him, it was a good investment! Because, I could make that back, and then I would be making that money forever.

Within six weeks of flying out to Atlanta for our consulting day, I held my first teleseminar that I ever held in this way, the way that he taught me.

In 67 minutes, I brought in $117,000 offering my Client Engagement System to lawyers, teaching them how to engage clients that come into their Law Firm.

Within six weeks, we did about $200,000 in sales of that product.

Then that, in 2007, went on to become what is now my *Personal Family Lawyer Program*, part of the 'Family Wealth Planning Institute'.

In 2008, that became its own $1,000,000+ business, and continued to 2009. Now, in 2010, we're in the midst of another massive transition with that business.

And, I can't say where it'll go from here. Because, we're at a turning point right now where it's either going to fail within the next couple of months. I shouldn't say fail. But, we're either going to say, "We can't realize the mission." Or, we're going to become a company that radically and completely transforms the way lawyers serve families, and small business centers, throughout the United States!

And we're *right there!* I'm in the midst of it right now! I can't tell you what's going to happen. Because, I don't know. What I *can* tell you is, that after about 6 months of a lot of questioning of myself, in terms of *'Ok, Alexis, now what do you want to do? Do you want to stick with this and build what you dreamed about building? Or, do you want to move on and make your next transition into the next thing?'*

I decided to commit to give this another 6 to 9 months to become what I had dreamed about it being. And if I can't do that, then I have a lot of other things that I want to do.

But, I feel like I need to finish this out first, and see where it can possibly go.

What has happened with this business is that I built a phenomenal coaching program and made lots of money. But, that wasn't ever my intention.

I didn't set out just to build the coaching program. I set out to radically transform the way that legal services are provided to families and small business owners!

And do that by teaching lawyers how to do it, and giving them not only the training, but the *technology* and the *tools* to do that!

So, we're going to see if I can do it… If I can't, then I have some other ideas in mind, some other plans. But, I'm going to see this one through, commit to it, and trust that just as it's always been in my life, the universe is guiding me and it's not steering me wrong!

RDY: So, you found a need and you filled it! But, at the same time, there's still only 24 hours in a day. So, you've got your family, and this horrific divorce, which we share that in common as well. And, your social life, and two 7-figure businesses, and your *sanity...*

For heaven's sake, how in the world did you find balance in all of that, so it wasn't like getting pulled in 12 different directions at once?

AMN: Wow! Well, I wouldn't call it *"Balance"!* Because, as a mom, and a business owner, I don't know that there's any such thing as real "Balance" like people call it on a daily basis.

What there is, is *Presence.* And that's something that I've cultivated really strongly over the past several years! It's the ability to be present with what I'm doing in that moment, and to eliminate the guilt. But, it's not completely eliminated by any means! But, it *is* very much reduced!

I reduced significantly the worry, the doubt, the fear, the things that pull me *out* of the present moment. So, in every moment, what I'm charging myself with is, *be here now. Be where you are right now!*

Trust that what you're doing is exactly what you're supposed to be doing, and that you're not supposed to be doing anything else...

So, when I'm with my kids, be with my kids. When I'm doing my work, do my work. And try not to think about one while I'm doing the other.

It's, of course, very, very difficult, very difficult!

For example, I was away last week, and now I'm here this week. Then, I'm going to be away again next week. Because, I'm going to L.A. to shoot some video.

Then, I'm actually going to a festival after we shoot the video, to reward myself. I'm going to take a few days purely for myself just to have fun!

So, my daughter said, "Mommy, I don't want you to go away." And that kills me inside!

At the same time though, I know that it's really important for me to be able to say to her, "I know, baby. Let's focus on being together now. We have this time together now. And I love being with you so much. I miss you so much when we're not together. And right now we *are* together! So, let's really enjoy the time that we have together now!"

So, I'm teaching my kids about how to have that presence for themselves. How not to worry about the future. And just be where they are right now. Because, what we're taught by historical patterns, and conditioning, and society is to not be where we are right now. To be worried about, 'Oh, she's leaving next week.' Or, 'Oh no! What's going to happen a few days from now?' Just be here now.

That is, to me, where the balance is!

Being able to be present in whatever you're doing in that moment. And not be feeling guilt, or worry, or doubt, or fear about what is coming in the next moment. And so that's what I focus on. That's the work that I do on a daily basis!

RDY: It's just so crazy! Those 3 little letters: "N-O-W" can completely redefine, and bring back into focus what it is that you need to be doing! As a matter of fact, in Buddhism, in movies and stuff, whenever people reach *Enlightenment*, there's like this glow around them. And they're floating and everything.

But, to Buddhists, *Enlightenment* is just being where you draw breath. It's right now. It's drawing breath in, and exhaling breath. And there's nothing more than that right there. When you said that you're focusing on NOW, that just rung so true in my ears. That I can't even describe it...I love that!

So, I know you can't go into detail on what you're working on like right this second. But, if the folks who are reading wanted to get more...They're reading that you're just like this *'Fearless Entrepreneurial Take No Prisoners Woman'!*

That you decide you want to do something, and then just seek, and go for it! And the *how* comes to you. If they want to learn more about this, what do they need to do? Where can they go?

AMN: So, if you're a lawyer, and you want to learn how to put in place the *New Paradigm Business Model* in your practice. The business model that results in your clients loving you, and you having free time to spend with your family, and you, really loving the practice of Law again, as a business owner...

You'll find more about that at: LawBusinessRevolution.com.

Right now, we have up there over $20,000 dollars of practice building resources that I paid over $20,000 dollars to have created for my own Law Firm. And I'm giving them to people for free!

We always have really great, useful, helpful content there that's going to help you make the transition to this new paradigm!

So, that's at: LawBusinessRevolution.com .

And, if you're not a lawyer, and you're a mom, or a Business Owner, or anybody else who's trying to figure out how to make this entrepreneurial life work, from a place of truth, and a place of awareness, a place of consciousness…And I don't mean like *Airy Fairy Consciousness*. I mean like real awake, aware, seeing what's right in front of you that you may not be looking at 'consciousness'…

You're going to find more on that at: AlexisMartinNeely.com

That's where I write about life, business, and the pursuit of truth.

RDY: Fantastic. You also have a book?

AMN: I have one book right now. It's called *Wear Clean Underwear*. It's a fast, fun, friendly, and essential guide to Legal Planning for Busy Parents. It's the #1 book on Legal Planning for Parents. So, if you're a parent, then you want to read my book *Wear Clean Underwear*.

I have another book for lawyers on the *New Paradigm Law Business Model*. And I'm working on a new book with lawyers called *More than Money: Creating a Legacy That Really Matters* that talks about how to really leave a legacy of your life! What *does* really happen when you die?

It's a bunch of lawyers talking about what the meaning of life is. What really happens when you die. How you can make sure that this life that you live is meaningful, not just while you're here, but after you're gone as well!

So, I'm working on that book now…Plus, I have about five other books I'm working on right now about the work I've created really helping these lawyers implement what I call the 'PFL Way of Doing Business'.

Then, I have another book I want to write called *The Road to Freedom*, and a few others that are on their way. But, they probably won't be out for a really long time.

RDY: Well, again, I know that you're super busy and I cannot thank you enough for taking the time to talk with me and contribute to this book.

AMN: Thank *you!* Once again, thank you *so* much for including me! It's been super fun! Any time that I can offer inspiration to anybody who's considering becoming an entrepreneur, or struggling in their entrepreneurial life, *this is the road to freedom!*

You *do* have choices and options! You *can* create your life exactly the way that you want it to be! You just have to get clear about how you want it to be, what you're willing to do in terms of being present in the moment, and just do exactly what needs to be done in *that* moment.

And then trusting that everything that's happening, everything that you're experiencing, is for your highest good! So, that you can become more of who you are in every moment!

So, thank you for reaching out to me, and I look forward to talking with you again.

RDY: Bye.

Jason Oman's comment on Alexis Martin Neely's chapter

It's really important to commit to doing just one little thing for yourself: Find something that makes you happy! If you need guidance to find out what that one thing might be, go get some. Because you truly DESERVE to be happy!

Plus, if you do this for yourself, it will show your children to do it for themselves as well. (Wouldn't it be great to create an entire generation of happy children? Think about what a different world that would create!)

So, when you decide to start your own business, it's important to commit to yourself to do something that will make you happy. Then follow through on that commitment no matter what challenges you face along the way.

Believe in yourself and in your ability to learn. Talk with other people who have done what you want to do, and do the same things they did to become successful!

Now, believe that you really CAN start & build a successful business and watch for opportunities to make it happen!

Chapter 6:

Terri Levine, the Coaching Guru

Rachel D. Young: Hi Terri! You've written a lot of books on selling and that's interesting. Because, most women that I know, don't like to sell. As a matter of fact, a lot of the woman I interviewed for this book said that, they vehemently don't like selling! So, why selling? Why do you like selling? Where did that come from?

Terri Levine: I guess it actually came from understanding that if you're going to be successful in business, as an entrepreneur, as the owner of a company, you have one job and one job only. And that job is truly to be doing marketing.

Marketing to me, has to do with being able to sell, being able to express what it is you do very clearly, and very plainly. I teach a really, really simple mindset. It's called 'Sell without selling.'

Because, I don't want to sell something to manipulate! I want to sell from a place of integrity, and love. The system is very simple. It's going to attract more clients, and more leads, than you've ever had before! It'll show you how to convert the right leads into paying clients or customers.

Then, how to retain those clients, or customers, long term. And how to 'Wow' them so they refer to you!

It really is a simple system. If people just stopped focusing on 'sell' as being a four letter word, then they will find that it's very easy to sell. They'll have more revenue, more business, more wealth, more prosperity, and be able to serve more people! In my view, that is what it's all about!

RDY: So, where did this come from? I mean, were you always this ambitious? Did you sell chocolate bars door to door?

TL: Honestly, it came initially from *Girl Scouts*. This is going to sound so funny! But, in *Girl Scouts*, I had to sell *Girl Scout Cookies*. And, this whole *Girl Scout Cookies* thing was just extremely stressful for me!

It was like, you know, how do you do this? I don't know what to do, or say. And we lived, at that time, in Yonkers, New York. I lived in a very, very large area, with apartment complexes.

And my mom said, "Just put on your uniform, and if people buy them, they buy them, and if they don't, they don't!"

That changed everything for me! Because, instead of worrying about, 'What am I supposed to say?' And, 'How am I supposed to say it and what am I supposed to do? I just very simply walked out and, with my uniform on like my mom suggested, I started to knock on doors. And started to say to people, "Would you like to have *Girl Scout* Cookies?"

And, I shared with them that my very, very *favorite* cookies, personally, were the mint ones. Still are the mint!

And I would say, "Would you like to buy any? Would you like to have some?"

And they would say, "Yes, I would." Or, "No" they wouldn't.

Or they would say, "Yes, I'll take a box."

And I would say, "Well, my mom puts them in the freezer, and they stay for a really long time, if you want that too!"

That's all I did. What I found was it was so, so simple to have people say, "Yes". And, it didn't bother me at all if anybody said "No".

I figured, maybe they don't like cookies. Maybe they don't like chocolate. Maybe they don't like *Girl Scouts*. Maybe they don't have money. I don't know. It just didn't matter. That's when I realized that, for me, the selling was actually ridiculously easy.

RDY: Wow. So, your mom turned it around, so it wasn't a personal rejection?

TL: Right. I mean, she just said, "Look. Just go out there with your uniform on. If they buy them, they buy them. And if they don't, they don't!" For me, as a kid, that just took all the pressure off! I had no worries, no fears. I just went out.

RDY: So, later on, farther down the line, you wound up getting a job. And you decided that wasn't for you. What caused the change there?

TL: I actually started out, out of college, in my own business. I had an Entrepreneurial Spirit. And, I started as a Speech Language Pathologist in my own business. That became very successful, and I sold that business.

I moved on to an Art Business that became very successful. Then, I sold that and I decided to get back into the field of 'Rehabilitation'. So, I worked as Vice President of Marketing for a company, and then President of a National Health Care Company.

I have to tell you, what I found is, that I was very good at those things.

I could create a whole lot of income, and a whole lot of money, and revenue for companies. And I was really, really good at that!

But, I also have to say that I was miserable, totally miserable! Because all I was doing was sitting in an office managing numbers, managing dollars. And, it just had something I totally did not enjoy! I didn't enjoy one Nano-second of it!

So, I eventually said, "You know, what I really enjoy is being out and about with all of the therapists all over the country."

So, instead of staying in the office, which is what my company really wanted me to do, I went out and I started doing these town meetings. Just being with people, and being with my therapist.

And they were getting more and more productive. And they were making more and more revenue. And productivity was going up and profits were going up.

You know, all the things we want!

I finally realized that I was doing this for another company. And I could have been doing it for myself! Doing something that I really, really loved!

So, I decided to move on, and it's one of these interesting things, Rachel, where you just never know where you are going to end up.

But, I'm on an airplane sitting next to someone and the gal says to me, "What do you do?"

And I say, "Oh, I work in this rehab business, blah, blah, blah."

Then, just to be polite, I say, "What do you do?"

She said, "I'm a coach." (Now, this is like 12 years ago, so, I had *no* concept that 'Coaching' was a profession.)

So, I blurted out, "What kind of team? What kind of sport?" Right? Because, I never heard of coaching. Never ever heard of it!

And she's like, "No. I'm a Business Coach."

I said, "A what?" And, it was a quick plane ride, just Philly to Boston. So, I mean you're in the air like 20 minutes. I mean, the whole ride is like 30 minutes. By the time I got off that plane I knew, in my heart, that I was meant to be a coach! I instantly looked into it and quit my J-O-B very, very shortly after that.

RDY: So, once you started doing it, did you have stumbles and pitfalls along the way? Or, were you one of those *few* where once you found it, and went for it, it was all smooth sailing?

TL: It was, almost every second of it, more than smooth sailing! I had 15 clients in 50 days, 30 clients in 30 more days, a waiting list, and I truly just never looked back! It was the right thing. I knew instantly that it was the right thing! I was just thrilled!

My clients were happy. I had freedom in my life. Not only was money rolling in, but I was just thrilled and delighted, every single second of my life was just fab! I mean, it was amazing! So, I had everything I ever dreamed about! Not just income, but doing what I loved, being with my family, vacationing.

The only bump in the road, over these 11 years or so, has been kind of a weird one. I had a sales person for one of my organizations who somehow, in her head, apparently thought *she* owned the company! So, I have had some litigation over that, which was just a little strange. But, everything else has been beyond smooth sailing! It's been joyful, and I get to work with the best clients on the planet! I really, really do!

RDY: Now, in talking about speaking at various organizations and places…I've done a lot of speaking as well. On Marketing, Information Marketing, and now with my new Weight Loss book. And, in the beginning, my presentation would be fine.

Then, when it came time to launch into the pitch, I would turn into like this robot. My voice would change. My body language would change.

Nothing about it was natural. Because, everything was always hammered to be, "Get them to the back of the room. Sell as much as you can. We really don't care what you say the first 60 minutes that you're talking anyway."

And, one day I was getting on stage. I wasn't feeling well. I didn't want to do the pitch thing the way that I had planned it.

Because I was told you have to memorize, you have to know every single word, and it has to be this perfectly choreographed reciting of, you know, what's going to get them to the back of the room. Because, there's only certain things that will do it.

And, I decided, you know what? I don't want to put on a show! I'm just going to go up there, and I'm just going to be myself. And I sold really well! From what I have studied about you, that wasn't coincidence, was it?

TL: No, not coincidence. Really not coincidence at all! This is kind of interesting for me. I was always on stage... When I was five years old, I was asked to speak in front of a school that was Kindergarten through 12th Grade.

So, there was a huge, huge audience of all the kids and all their parents. I just got up there and I spoke, and I didn't think it was any big deal. And people were like, "Are you nervous? Do you have butterflies?"

I'm like, "What would I be nervous about? What would I have butterflies for?" Like I never understood that. So, being on stage, for me, is very natural, presenting on stage.

Where it got a little messed up, to be honest with you, is that people were trying to teach me how to pitch from the stage.

That's *not* natural to me! I'm not a pitch person. I really believe that if I can go out there, and just create value, value, value. And then give people the opportunity to know what it would be like to work with me, or take home my products or services, then if they want it, they will raise their hand and they've got it.

If not, then, as long as I have delivered a lot of value, I feel really good about that! So, that really is part of the 'sell without selling' formula.

It's just offering what I call 'Your gifts'. Sharing your gifts with the world. Giving to give. Not putting on that show. But, being yourself, being in integrity, being authentic, and being who you are.

And that is why you sold really well. You sold really well because you were being who you are!

But, it's been an interesting journey for me, Rachel, in having trained with some of the top sales people, and what I will call 'Pitch people', and 'Persuasion people'. Basically trying it all on and saying, "No, that's not me!"

What *is* me, is just being me. And now, I know how I want to be, and who I want to be on stage. And it works great for me!

RDY: Now, I'm hearing this throughout our call…One of your platinum coaching students said that you were, and this is her quote, "Tough with love."

Can you be a passive entrepreneur and still reach that seven figure, millionaire status?

TL: That's an interesting question. Well, I would say 'No'.

You can't be passive, in terms of, I really believe that as the entrepreneur you have to be out there. You have to be marketing. You have to be spreading the word, whether it's on stage, in teleclasses, on the phone, in person. You have to be out there.

The 'attraction' comes from who you are, and being out in the world. So, #1 always for me, is that you must be in front of people in some way, shape or form. But, I do sort of chuckle about that. I'm tough with love. Do you know what I mean?

I'm just kind of smiling about that. I can't be passive. Because I really wouldn't be a good coach. So, I couldn't say to my clients, "Oh, that's ok, or rah, rah, rah". Because, they're not going to get the results. Then, if they don't get the results, not only are they unhappy, but I have a guarantee that they make $100,000 dollars in their first year learning from me! Not a lot of people are willing to give people that kind of guarantee!

I know my stuff works. And I know that, if they do it, it's a piece of cake. So, I give that guarantee.

But, I can't sit back then and say, "Oh, you didn't do anything this week. Well, that's ok, honey. I understand."

I have to be... while I *am* compassionate, I have to be tough. And say, "You're operating a *Business!* You need to feed your family. You need to focus on what's important!"

In my experience, you can't be what you referred as a 'Passive entrepreneur', and make it to millionaire status. I don't even know if you'll make it to six-figure status. Because, you have to be marketing your business!

You're not in the business of Speaking, Training, Coaching, Mentoring, Real Estate, or whatever you are in. You're in the business of *marketing, speaking, coaching* Real Estate, or whatever your retail store is.

Does that make sense? You're in the 'Marketing' and 'Coaching' business

RDY: Oh, absolutely, absolutely.

Now, in your book, *Coaching for Everyone*, you talk about discovering your true purpose and your mission in life. So, I have three questions for you about that.

First, as woman, (and me speaking as a Southern Woman), a lot of us are bred to have kids, be a good mom, and a good wife. And, to do anything other than those things, even in today's society, creates this sense of guilt that we're not doing what we're supposed to be doing…

If you're working on growing your business, then you're taking time away from your children.

If you're spending time with your children, you could be growing your business.

You're never in the one place that you need to be, at the one time you need to be there.

How do you know for certain that what you are doing is the path you are supposed to take in life? And is there just one path?

TL: This is a really good question! I don't believe that there is *one* path! I don't think we were put on the planet to do one particular thing, nor to meet the one particular person.

I think we're put here to go forth, to share our gifts, talents, and experiences, meet a lot of people and create as much value as we can. So, I look at, particularly women, because we grow up with so many *shoulds* and we get that guilt…

Well, I'm supposed to be a good mom, supposed to be home with my kids. But, I also want to run a business, and be good for all these *supposed to's* and *should do's*.

And, what I basically say is, what is it that's very important to you in life? In other words, 'If the world were going to end tomorrow, what would you be doing?' And, if you say, "That's just being home with my kids." Well, then maybe *that* is what you need to do.

But, if you say, "Well, I would like to spend time with my kids, and I would also like to do this for my client, or be in my store part of the time or whatever it is," then that is your answer.

So, what I say to people is if it's all based on 'should, should, should', the first thing you need to do is do the research about how much better parenting is going now that women are actually more active in the workforce. And that kids are growing up with a better blend, and an understanding of that word that nobody really understands called "Balance" is all about. So, it gives you an opportunity to really model having a great life for your kids.

So, this is what I believe. I believe the only way that you really know what your path is in life, is to constantly do 'Self-Coaching'.

That is really why I wrote *Coaching is For Everyone*. It's really a book about 'Self-Coaching' and how to do it. I think the *Supposed To Be's* are what is in your heart! We all have that little voice in our heart and our heads. So, I asked myself. *'Is this what I really chose to do? Does this feel good?'*

When I even look at a Client Application, I say:

Would it be joyful to work with this person?
Would this support my values, their values?
Can I really add value to them?

So, I think these are important kinds of questions. And I don't think there is just one path, Rachel. I think if I chose to stay in *Speech Language Pathology*, I would've given that my all. And I'm certain I would have made a great career out of it. Same with the Art Business.

I just heard that little voice within me saying, *'There are other gifts that you have. Share them!'*

RDY: Question #2 - What do you do if you have taken the 'wrong path'?

TL: Oh, that is a great question! I've had lots of client who were there. And, first, let me say this is how you know that you are there...

You literally have what I call the "Sunday night dreads", for example… You don't want to get up in the morning and go to your business. You just dread going in. You don't want to open the computer. You don't want to answer the phones. It's like, "Oh, I just don't want to do this!"

That is the wrong path.

That was me, by the way, at the end of my experience in the world of corporate.

We'll call it that.

I would literally not want to get up in the morning. I would hate waking up. I would drive to the office and think I would rather be doing anything but this.

And so, in my heart, I knew that that was no longer what... I might be good at it, which I was, but it was no longer what made me happy as a human being.

So, what do you do?

First, you notice that you've taken the wrong path.

Second, you go back and you figure out what you're passionate about.

Your business really should be your passion!

So, how do you want to make a difference in the world? What are your gifts? What can you add to world? What is easy, and natural, and effortless for you? What kind of value can you add?

Then you get on the right path. And you don't waste another nanosecond! Because life is too short!

We never know when our *checkout date* is.

You could be leaving the planet tomorrow.
And not that I want that to happen to anyone. But, that is why I say you need to live each minute, each second *in the moment* getting all the juice!

RDY: Yes. I love that! I feel like a lot of the women that are reading this book have wanted to do more than just the 9 to 5, than just the Stay-At-Home mom, than just the College Student…

They wanted to do more for a long time. But, they may be afraid of making a mistake or failing. And I think that's probably true across the board, for any entrepreneur, but especially women. Can you talk about failing for a while?

TL: Oh, this is such a good topic! And I'm glad we are discussing it! I really believe that women in particular have a lot of fear.

They're afraid of making a mistake.
They're afraid of failing.
They're afraid people will laugh at them, they will ridicule them.
They're afraid people will say, "I knew you wouldn't be able to do that!"

You see, we grow up with a lot of that. And a lot of this is biological.

It's just sort of an inherent thing that we have, and as much as I'm not sexist... There are biological differences that we cannot overlook. And one of them is that women have a lot of fear about failing, very deep concerns.

Men are used to being cut from things. They're used to being cut from the baseball team. You know, they didn't make the football squad. And they just sort of get used to that. And they figure out another thing to go on to, and they roll with it.

Women, in my experience, and I have coached like 5000 people worldwide, and I see this as a pattern…They have big things that they want to do. They have big dreams. But, they don't honor those dreams. They keep the dreams almost stuffed within them. Because they're afraid to share them. Because, either, people would laugh at them, or they're never going to really do them, and people would think they're silly. And that's a big concern that they have.

You see, in our society women aren't taken as seriously as men.

So, let me just share with you…When I went to quit my J.O.B., I told males in my life, who said, "Are you kidding me?" You know, "Good luck. Is there anything I can do for you?"

They kind of looked at me with a very skeptical eye, but didn't discourage me and say, you know, "Don't do it."

The women in my life all said, "That's ridiculous. You shouldn't do it. You're president of a company. You make a lot of money. You're young." You know, "I would do anything to have what you have, to have your success," they said.

And I said, "But, I'm not happy. I don't have a life. I don't see my family. I don't go on vacations. I don't have freedom." And they said, "Well, you know, that would be so gutsy to quit."

So, here's the thing that I say, particularly to women, but to everyone…"The fear is real and I don't believe we should try and get rid of the fear. I believe we should just notice it, ok?" The same with losing weight.

A lot of people, you're an expert on this, a lot of people actually want to lose weight. But, they're also afraid of failing. Or, they get the weight off and they're afraid it won't stay off, and then people will ridicule and make fun of them. And do you know what? In life, we just have to take chances. We just have to go for what our dreams and passions are.

My girlfriend Marny, died when she was 40, of breast cancer. And what was very tragic, obviously losing her so young was tragic. What else was tragic is all she did was work, work, work, work, but, not really at the dream in her heart.

So, I just say to people, "Listen. What is more fearful? Going to your grave, which could be in any moment, having never given what you have to give, or experience, or going through your life by rote, not enjoying it?"

I say, "Go give it a shot. What's the worst thing that can happen?" That is my favorite self-coaching question! *What is the worst thing that can happen?* When I quit my job, I didn't know that I would do well as a coach. I didn't.

So, I was like, "What is the worst thing that could happen?" Well, I could be a Speech Pathologist.

Well, what is the worst thing that could happen? I'm sure I could get hired at McDonalds.

What's the worst thing that could happen? I could babysit.

What's the worst thing that could happen? I could dog sit.

I wouldn't let my dream die. And, that's what you need to do! Just step up to the plate and take a swing at the ball! And, do you know what?...If you miss it, you should be the first one laughing. Because, honestly, it's not as important as everybody thinks it is!

RDY: Wow. So, going back to something you just said earlier, about coaching is for everyone. You said, that it was about self coaching.

I'm a pretty voracious reader. And, whenever I hear 'Self-Coaching', that's like the first thing that I think of. To just learn everything you can on a subject. Can you talk about Self-Coaching? And how do you know, as a coach, if you're worth a crap?

TL: That's a great question! *That* is a really good question! So, I will first of all address *self-coaching*. And then, I will get to the other piece.

To me, I think the biggest gift I got in going through Coach Training, was that *I* was changing! As I was learning coaching skills, I was thinking differently.

I was feeling differently. I was behaving differently. And, everything in my life changed! So, for me, weight fell off of me! No diet, no exercise, the weight just fell off!

Relationships got better and better. Freedom came into my life. Spirituality, which I never had. A very close community of friends. Things I had never really had in my life! And it all came from Self-Coaching. And really asking myself Self-Coaching questions. Even when I was going to eat something…

Instead of just shoving something into my mouth, I would say, "Am I really in the mood for this cookie? Is this the best chocolate chip cookie I can have? Or, would I like to wait another day where I can get a fresh one at a bakery, instead of one out of a bag? How much of this cookie do I want to eat?"

So, I would constantly be asking myself internal questions, and getting new and different answers. I also became more outgoing, just because I was losing my fear!

Then, how do we know if we are... I love how you said that, 'worth a crap?' The way I judge this for myself, as a coach, is 100 percent by client results! I give my clients the tools, the skills to go to seven figures and beyond, working 2 to 3 days a week.

That's what I'm gifted at! I'm good at one thing on the planet! *That* is my one thing, and I am really, really good at! That is the only thing I can say that about... really, in the world. That is what Terri Levine is really good at!

So, for me, I know that I'm worth a crap, because they give me raving reviews. Testimonials. Many of my clients have been with me for more than 10 years. They refer and refer. They stay. They come back.

I have one client, she was with me for two hours. She made $15,000 dollars. Another client spent a day with me last week, $26,000 dollars. Another client spent a whole day at my home, $96,000 dollars.

And I could go on and on. So, I believe I'm worth a crap, because I create real results! Not airy fairy. Not sort of. Or kind of, my stomach feels better, and I *think* I'm happier. But, real solid concrete results!

RDY: Great! I have a question for you that I also asked of Kendra Todd. It involves Gordon Ramsey, the Hell's Kitchen Guy…And, he was saying on his show that the thing that he loves about what he's doing is, that every day is different, you know? He's got all of these restaurants, all of these shows…

Even when he has hit what he defined as 'Success', every day is still different! And that's what keeps him going! That's what prevents him from stopping everything, and just retiring, and going off to enjoy his money…

How do *you* define success? And, how do you know when it's time to wrap it up?

TL: Interesting question! Success for me is very personal. It's having joy at what you do. It's not money. It's having joy at what you do, and having fulfillment!

Fulfillment in that I know that I'm creating value for people, and giving them my gifts. It's fulfillment that people are happy with what they're receiving. It's fulfillment in that I want to get up in the morning, and go to work, and after vacations, I can't wait to get back to work!

It's fulfillment in every single day having time and freedom to be with my friends, and family. Or to just take a walk, or smell the air, or go on vacation. And it's also some financial, in terms of being able to do things in my life without worry, or without thinking about, 'Oh, that would be hard. I would like to have that, but that would be difficult.'

Just financially being very free, being able to give money to my charity, a foundation I have for children with RSD. Being able to give money to nieces, nephews, family, friends, whoever needs it.

Those are the factors, to me, that make me feel, 'Yes, I'm successful in my life and in my business.'

The interesting part of your question to me is, 'How do you know when it's time to call it *Quits*?' I've actually coached some clients to call it *'Quits'*. Because they're bored. They're tired of work. Or, of their clients.

Or, they don't really want to go to the office. Or, the thought of turning on the computer is dull. Or, they talk a lot about being on vacation, vacation, vacation when they just came back from vacation, and that's what they're looking forward to again already!

So, to me, we need to take a look at things like that, and I notice for those things for myself on a regular basis as well. Every Friday I have a meeting with myself, and I say:

Am I happy?
Am I rejoicing in what I'm doing?

Is it still joy-filled?
And, am I creating value?

And, if my answer is 'Yes', I just keep doing what I'm doing. And, at any point in time, if for whatever reason it's 'No', then I'll do something else, and move on.

It's very easy, I believe, if you're really paying attention, to be able to do those kinds of things. Just really pay attention to: Are you still resonating and having a blast?

RDY: So, what is next for you? Because, I know you've written umpteen books. I mean, they're all over Amazon. What's next in the pipeline?

TL: I don't want to write books right now. I've just been asked by a publisher to write a couple of books. And I said, "Not right now." I feel like, where I'm impacting people in a big way is my VIP program.

In addition, I find that when I'm on stages, and I'm in front of audiences, that that is where I make the most impact! I can take an audience, and literally just transform them, from where they came in, to where they leave!

So, for me, it's touching and impacting more people through speaking to them and being with them. So, that's what's on the horizon for me. And I will say, that one of the things I love to do is just stay open and see what else flows in! It's fun to do that!

RDY: Wow. Well, I'm excited to see and hear and share with everyone all of the great things that you have going on! I really appreciate that you took the time with me!

TL: It's been fun! And you asked some *very* interesting questions! And, if we can continue to impact women, in business, and help them make the kind of money that they deserve, I'm all over that!

RDY: Awesome. Fantastic. Thanks so much, Terri!

TL: You're welcome! This has been a blast, and I'm glad we did this!

Jason Oman's comment on Terri Levine's chapter

Sales and selling has to be done from a place of integrity and love. It can NOT be done successfully using manipulation.

Don't be afraid to fail. Just get up, go out and do what you want to do in terms of starting your own business. If you need to, start small, but start *something*!

If you have big dreams; honor them. Do something that will feed your dreams. Get out there and share those dreams. Find the joy in what you do. Find your fulfillment in creating value in the eyes of other people. Give of your gifts and talents and you will reap the rewards you so richly deserve, both monetarily and in your own feelings of self-worth.

Take some time to think about how you could best impact other people's lives yourself. More millionaires have been created from positively impacting other people's lives than virtually any other way!

Chapter 7:

Sydney Biddle Barrows, Former Mayflower Madam

Rachel D. Young: Probably known to millions as *'The Mayflower Madam'*, Sydney Biddle Barrows has a unique success story, but I'm going to let her tell the story herself.

But, as you may have guessed from her nickname, she ran a very exclusive and extremely successful Call Girl Service named *Cache* in New York City.

Now, her service was kind of small, but very upscale.

In fact, *Cache* prospered for about five and a half years until New York's finest shut it down. But later, officials publicly conceded that it was the most honest and professionally run business of its kind to ever operate in New York City!

'Oh my!' Right?

So, the tabloids were in 'Media Heaven' over this story! There's sex. There's High Society clients who were celebrities. I mean, we're talking like Arab sheiks, and business men. And, I bet if she did some name dropping today, you would clearly know who she was talking about! Now, her first book *A Mayflower Madam* went straight to the top of the *New York Times* Best Seller list!

It was also made into a TV movie starring Candace Bergen! So, Sydney has been on like every morning television show that exists!

I mean, we're talking like Larry King, Phil Donohue. She has been on Oprah several times! As well as several other talk shows over the years! She was even featured in her own A&E biography! And she co-hosted *Saturday Night Live* with Candace Bergen! How cool is that?

She has not only done guest lecturing at colleges all over the U.S.. But, she's done speaking engagements at Ivy League schools like Brown, and Columbia, and for clients like the *Young Presidents Organization*!

She has an active consulting practice.

She's probably the most unlikely source of any 'Cutting-Edge' business strategies that you're going to read in this book!

But, for those of you who are thinking, "Oh, my business is different." You probably think you can't learn anything from a former madam…

Well, you need to pay attention to her right now! Because, you're actually going to hear what *your* business and *'The World's Oldest Profession'* have in common…

Sydney, thank you for joining me today!

Sydney Biddle Barrows: Thank you so much, Rachel.

RDY: Now, I'm just going to jump right to it. Because, I know the first question on my mind and probably everybody reading is: How did a nice girl like you grow up to become a *Madam*?

SBB: Well, it certainly isn't something that I planned! It's not your world's most 'normal' career path. And, you better believe… It isn't something my parents planned!

I literally fell into it! I'll try and make a long story as short as I can…

I started out in retail, on the executive training program, at a now defunct store called Abraham and Strauss. Which, at the time, was the jewel in the crown of the late Federated Department Stores.

I started out in the bath shop and then I went to fine jewelry and watches. I used to say I went from toiletries to diamonds.

Then, I went to a small resident buying office where I ended up getting fired. Because, I refused to participate in a Kick Back Scheme. So, there I am on the Unemployment Line.

You can tell this is a long time ago. Because you actually had to go stand in line to get Unemployment. Unlike these days, when you can just sit down at your computer and do it all.

I met another gal who was also unemployed for a number of different reasons. But, we started hanging out together.

Because, you know, being unemployed can be pretty darn lonely. So, one day, it's my turn to go to her house.

She lives in Greenwich Village. I walk into her apartment, and there she is, unpacking a brand new stereo.

Well, I didn't know she had money. She was making I think it was 150 dollars a week, the same as I was. And I wasn't in the business of buying any new stereos.

So, of course, I wanted to know where she got it. I'm asking her and she was kind of hemming and hawing…

Finally, I said, "Well, you know, did it fall off the back of a truck?" I mean, "can I get one, too?"

Finally she looked at me, and she was very serious, and she said, "Sydney, do you swear that you won't tell anybody?"

I said, "I swear."

She said, "I answer the phones for an escort service."

I said, "Oh, what's an escort service?"

I mean, seriously. I didn't have a clue. I had never heard the term before. So, when she started explaining to me what it was, I was like horrified!

She was talking about prostitutes. Oh, my, I know somebody who knows a prostitute! I asked all the questions I think that everybody reading this would ask. I mean, I was horrified. But, I was fascinated!

And because I was the only person who knew she was doing this, over the next few months, she would tell me all about it.

You know, all she was doing was answering the phones. And it didn't sound like anyone was holding a gun to any of these girl's heads or anything…

Anyway, one day, she called me up and she said, "You know, Sydney, one of the girls in the office is leaving. Would you be interested in the job?"

Well, you know, all of the sudden I had cold feet. I was afraid of the police. I was afraid of the mafia. I didn't want to get involved in something like this.
But, it did pay 50 dollars of the books. And 150 dollars a week doesn't get you very far in New York City, even back then.

So I thought, maybe it wouldn't hurt to go over there for the interview.

So, I go over there for the interview and, you know, I get a chance to meet some of the girls who were every bit as nice as my girlfriend had told me. You know, I got a chance to hear some of the clients on the speaker phone.

They certainly seemed like perfectly decent guys. So I thought, you know, it's just answering the phone. I think I will do it! So, I took the job.

Well, it was very obvious from the first night I was there that while this may have been the world's oldest profession; he was not running it very professionally.

I mean, my girlfriend and I were constantly Monday morning quarterbacking.

You know, '*he should be doing it this way. Why doesn't he do it that way?*' You know, '*if it were me, I would do this?*'

So, eventually we just sort of looked at each other and said, you know, "we're at least as smart as he is. We're definitely nicer than he is. Why don't we start our own escort service?" And so we did. I mean, that is really how it started. I literally just fell into it.

RDY: I'm sitting here and my eyes are the size of saucers right now as you're telling this! Now, the next logical question in this is, how did you go from escort service to just having published a book *Uncensored Sales Strategies,* which is one of my favorite books of all time, by the way!

How did you go from madam to authoring a book with Dan Kennedy, and now super successful business woman?

SBB: Well, I hate to be repetitive. But, the real answer is… I fell into that, too!

After my first book *Mayflower Madam* hit #1 on the *New York Times* Best Seller List, as you said before. I started being asked to speak at different places. Which absolutely floored me!

I just couldn't believe that all these people were asking me to speak and they all wanted me to talk about business, primarily marketing.

So, one of my biggest clients was the *Young Presidents' Organization.* And what would happen is, after I would give my speech, people would come up to me and they would ask me if I did consulting.

Well, I didn't know what consulting was any more than I knew what an escort service was when I first heard about it!

But, I could tell they were willing to pay me money to do it. And that was interesting to me. So, I started asking questions. You know, sort of, well, "What is it you need help with?"

"What is it you're hoping I can do for you?"

You know, just questions to try and figure out what the hell this whole consulting thing was all about. What were they expecting of me? And I remember one guy in particular was very explicit. I was thinking to myself, 'I can do that.'

So, I agreed to do it. And, as you can imagine, I'm sure almost everybody reading has had this exact same experience…

I was absolutely terrified that I was going to be found out as the most incredible fraud.

You know, here I am taking all this money to go and tell…
I mean, I was scared shitless to be honest with you!
So, I get there and it was just so obvious that there were all these different things that just weren't right.

I thought that was an anomaly. So it really took me 3 or 4 digs, before I realized that a lot of people didn't know what the hell they were doing. And that I just had this... everyone has got a gift, Rachel.

Your gift, for instance, is copyrighting. My gift is not technology. I'm real technologically blonde!

But, I really do have a gift for seeing the incongruence walking in the door of somebody's business, and seeing the incongruence between what they say, and who they say they are, who they want, or say their client is, and the way they're actually running their business. Because you're in your own business every day!

You walk in that door, and you just don't see things with *Fresh Eyes*. In other words, things someone who has never been there before, would see. People are really amazed!

I remember one of my very first clients… A very, very upscale spa. I walk up to the front door, and there is all this graffiti, horrible graffiti right next to the door.

This is like a very upscale spa! Not only that, but you could tell it had been there for a while. Because it was kind of chipping off. It wasn't brand new.

Do you know what? They were so used to seeing it every day, that they just didn't even notice it!

But, what a jarring thing for a brand new client to see when they're coming somewhere! Where they're hoping to be made more beautiful and they're going to be end up spending a lot of money to do that! And they walk into a place that has graffiti all next to the door!

Oh, and then, oh, it gets even better, Rachel!

One of the girls at the front desk had a purple streak in her hair, a ring in her nose, and was wearing the nastiest black high tops, Ked's sneakers, that I've ever seen in my whole life!

Now, those two things are very incongruent with being a very upscale business where you are charging people a lot of money to do what it is that you do!

And that's just for starters!...

So, that is what I do. I go in with fresh eyes. A lot of times I do a mystery shop… I go in and I pretend to be a client, or a patient. I have a lot of doctors, mainly cosmetic surgeons, and dentists, and dermatologists. And it's just amazing what I find! And I really love it!

Because it's just it is fun for me to be able to, like, get their act together. And to make everything be what it's supposed to be. And be congruent. And really tell their story, and get across their brand, and their image, and their story. That's what I do!

RDY: Now, in reading your book, one of the things that was probably the biggest eye opener for me, is that you give credit to learning lessons from other successful businesses!

One of the stories you tell in your book has to do with one of the things that you did in *Cache* that truly helped create that experience...

I hope you don't mind. But, I would love if you would share the champagne story.

SBB: Our first year in business, when Christmas time came around, we were looking for something to do for our clients to thank them.

You know, our good clients, not everybody. But, our regulars, you know, to make them feel special and to thank them and that sort of thing.

At first, we thought, well, we'll just give them a free hour or something.

But, it's never a good idea to give away something that you expect people to pay you for! Not only that, but it would 've cost us a small fortune. Because we would have still had to pay the girl. So, we nixed that idea.

Then, we came up with the idea of, why don't we give everybody a bottle of really expensive champagne? And, at the time, Dom Perignon was the most expensive and most exclusive non-vintage champagne you could buy.

So, we went to Sherry Leaman, and we ordered two cases of Dom Perignon. And when a client would call any time between Thanksgiving and the end of January, we would have the girl swing by the office first, and pick up a bottle of chilled champagne, and take it with her on the call.

I got this idea from a cosmetics company. Now, cosmetics companies sell products. I was in the service business. So, one of the points I want to make is that you need to look at everybody who is successful, and see, if you can adopt what they do for your business…

One of the reasons, for anyone reading who doesn't know what 'Gift with purchase' is… Every once or twice a year, every cosmetics company, not all at the same time, of course, they offer… usually it's a cute, some kind of cute little bag with maybe six or eight different products in there in little miniature sizes usually. And you can get that for free if you purchase say, $40, $50, $60, whatever, worth of their product...

And this does several things for the cosmetics company...

First of all, it increases your transaction size! Because usually someone has to buy more than... like, if you go in there for a lip-liner pencil, and it's only $18, and the gift is $30, well, you're going to spend another $12 to get that gift that you wouldn't have spent otherwise. So, that is the transaction size.

The second thing it does is, it gives them the opportunity to put in front of potential clients things they make that the customer might not have otherwise tried.

For instance, it has got to be 20 something years ago... I got a little vial of perfume called "Knowing" from Este Lauder in one of their little... I am still using it.

So, that one little vial. I can't tell you how many hundreds of dollars over all these years the people have made from me.

Giving them the champagne did the same thing for me, too. It, first of all, it upped our transaction size. Because nobody guzzles Dom Perignon.

So, if the client was a one hour... usually the one hour client, she would usually end up being there for two hours. If he was a three hour client, she would usually end up being there for four hours. You know, that kind of thing. We would almost always get an extra hour out of it.

So, that upped our transaction size from making... you know, it made us and, of course, the young lady, very happy.

The next thing it did was it said to the client, "We think you're so special that we have gone out and made it a point to give you the most expensive, the most exclusive, the best champagne that we could find!"

What this said to them is, "Oh, they must think that I'm the best. They must really value me because they are giving me such an incredible gift!"

And what it also does is, it emphasizes our prestige. Because we were a 'Prestige Business'. And here we are giving away a very prestigious gift!

And that's a mistake a lot of businesses make. They give away something that doesn't reflect who they are. And this is a big, big, big mistake!

You want to always give away a gift that emphasizes who you are, that reflects who you are, and that sort of thing.

Another thing it did is, it created an experience. Actually more than one experience for the client. First of all, he had the experience of feeling really thrilled, and exited, and happy that he got this wonderful gift. And that we thought so highly of him. Then, he had the experience of sitting there drinking the most expensive champagne with a beautiful woman! And, third of all, all of my young ladies had to carry in their handbags a packet of bubble bath.

So, those women out there who have never heard of a champagne bubble bath, it doesn't mean you bathe in champagne. What it means is, you sit in a bubble bath drinking champagne with a member of the opposite... well, it could be a member of any sex that you're into.

So, I have 100 dollars that said every single client who had that experience whenever they think of champagne, or whenever they think of bubble baths, they go back and they remember that incredible experience that they had! Because a lot of people have heard about having champagne bubble baths, but you try and find someone who has actually done it. Well, I gave my clients that experience!

So, that's what I learned from another business, that was nothing like my business! And, as I said before, I hate to repeat myself. But, I think this is so important…

Is everyone should look at what other businesses are doing that is successful. And see if there's a way that they can model it for their business.

RDY: I love that story! Ok so, I'm sitting here thinking as you're talking and a lot of advertising and marketing campaigns tend to focus on the product, or the service, that they're trying to sell, right? But, I can tell from the champagne story, you make the argument that it's just as important for an ad to repel certain customers.

But, that's a concept you don't really hear talked about a whole lot. Can you talk a little bit about that?

SBB: Yeah, I think the reason for that is, most people like to think that everyone is their customer. But, when you try to be everything to everyone, you end up being nothing to no one! Or, you end up being something to just a few people who don't really care all that much!

The more you *niche* yourself, the more money you can charge. The more loyalty you will have. But, that is something that we can get into later...

Anyway, the only place we could advertise when we first opened up was a publication run by Al Goldstein. And some men reading this may have heard of, the name of the publication was called *Screw*.

And if you think the name is tacky, I assure you it was the classiest thing about it.

Anyway, there was a whole section of ads for 'Ladies for Hire' basically. The ads were just unbelievably tacky! I mean they were so busy. They were so vulgar.

One of my favorites, that I always remember, was there was a drawing of a gal sitting there with her legs in a big V, and the headline was, "See you M into my valley."

So, this is what we were up against. We created the most gorgeous ad!

First of all, there were huge amounts of white space which was unlike everybody else. There was so much white space that our ad literally leaped off the page!

It had a heavy black border around it, and a sort of narrower black border inside, and the only thin in the ad was the name of the business, *Cache*. And our tag line, which was 'New York's most trusted service.'

And trust, believe me, this is something that is very much *not* in the picture in the escort service business.

Then it gave the amount of money we were charging which, at the time... what did we start out as?

I forget if we started out at $100 or $125, it has been so long. Whatever it was, it was a lot more than everyone else was charging!

Then it just gave our hours, which was, you know, five in the afternoon until one in the morning.
Everyone else was open 24 hours a day, and they all made it a real point to let you know that. And then it gave our phone numbers.

Now, what this ad said to people was, first of all, unless you're willing to spend a lot of money, don't call us.

Unless you're someone who is employed during the day, and you're not out late at night. You know, partying and doing drugs and all that stuff.

If you're someone who has to get up in the morning, you know, we aren't sending you somebody real late because we didn't... I didn't want those kinds of clients.

I wanted guys who had to get up in the morning, because they had a business meeting. You know, they had to be in bed by one in the morning, two in the morning.

Because they had to get up the next day.

So, I didn't want the kind of clients that, you know, wanted to see someone at three in the morning.

And it just... you could just tell from the ad that the kinds of young ladies that we would have were going to be a very sort of 'Up Scale' classy, young ladies.

Now, there are a lot of guys who don't want that. I mean, remember Hugh Grant? When he was going out with Elizabeth Hurley, he went and picked up that street hooker?

I forget what her name was, remember in Los Angeles?

And people said, "Wait a second. This guy has Elizabeth Hurley, one of the most beautiful women on the planet and he is out there picking up that?"

Well, there are a lot of guys who are turned on by tacky and trashy.

So, we have to make it very clear that that was not the business that we were in!

Then, of course, the minute somebody called us and we answered the phone, you could just tell by the way the young lady who answered the phone spoke to them and it was very important the way they spoke to us.

I mean, if someone said to us, "Yeah, what do you got tonight?" the answer was a click.

But, if someone said to us, "Hi, my name is Mr. So and so. I'm staying at the Waldorf. I was just wondering if you could tell me a little something about your service."

Well, this is the kind of guy we're looking for. Do you know what I mean? He has some manners. He knows how it works. He's probably somebody who is going to be nice to the young ladies. Which, of course, is very important to us.

That's what I mean about attracting and repelling certain clients. That is very important!

You don't want to waste your time, or your employees time, talking to people who aren't going to buy from you. Because they can't afford what you sell. They aren't really in the market for what you sell.

You've got a lot of 'Lookie Lous' out there. So, you want to try and get rid of the Lookie Lous. Because, you don't want to waste your time on them. So, you know, certain advertising and marketing can help you with that.

RDY: Now, I notice that you emphasize, a bit more than I think other people have, that it's crucial for people to ask "What business am I *really* in?"

Any solopreneur, entrepreneur, business owner, anyone with a professional practice like an attorney or a doctor, has to ask themselves that question!

Or, you know, *"What is it that my customers, or clients, or patients, what do they really want to buy from me?"* I think that's **crucial**!

Because, a lot of folks just assume that the business they're in is the business that they're in. If that makes sense, you know? What do you mean by that? Why is that so important?

SBB: Well, you're absolutely right when you say a lot of people think, 'Well, the business I'm in is the business I'm in.'

But, as an example, a Cosmetic Dentist is *not* in the 'Tooth-Drilling Business'. They're in the *'Give me the confidence, so when I smile people don't see my crooked teeth'* business! They're in the *'We're going to help you not feel embarrassed any more because of your smile'* business! They're in the business of *'Somebody has gotten a divorce, and they want to look good'* business…

That divorced person is going back out there into the marketplace. So, the dentist is in the *'Give me confidence and make me attractive'* business.

Now, some dentists are *not* in the 'Tooth-Drilling' business. Some are, but a lot of people aren't.

Now, if I were to say to you, "Rachel, what business do you think I was really in?" You would probably say to me, "Oh, come on, Sydney, you were in the *sex* business. I mean isn't it obvious?"

And yes, it's true that sex was involved. But, that was **_not_** the business that I was really in. The business I was really in was the *'Fantasy'* Business!

If someone just wanted sex, I assure you they could have gotten it for a hell of a lot less! We were charging them top dollar! And what they were paying for was not sex. Although, honestly, that *was* a part of it.

But, they were paying for the experience they had from the minute they dialed our number until the young lady walked out of their door.

My clients were looking for the High Class, most expensive New York call girl to walk into their hotel room or apartment. And having no other agenda other than pleasing them.

You know… laughing at their jokes, just listening to them go on and on about whatever it is, and acting like they're interested, which actually these guys were *very* interesting so that wasn't too difficult.

You know, these girls never had a headache. They never had a 'Bad day at the office.' The client could basically lay back, and not have to do anything.

Which, back then, when the whole 'Women's Lib' thing was really going on, some men were like, you know, 'What about me? What about ours? You have to satisfy me!' There were a lot of guys who didn't want to have to do that all the time.

So, with a Call Girl, you could do that. Because what you were doing to satisfy her makes her happy. You are giving her the money. So, there were a lot of different reasons and a lot of different fantasies that clients had when they called us. So, that's why we were really in the 'Fantasy' Business, not the 'Sex' business.

Because, as I said before, if that was all they wanted, they could have gotten it a zillion other places for a hell of a lot less!

RDY: So, ok... this is the thing that I've been waiting to ask you. It's this question…

We all know that people sell a lot more when they give a good guarantee, right? That's just common knowledge. But, you offered a guarantee within your former business! How on earth do you guarantee a 'Call Girl'?

SBB: Yeah, this is something a lot of people don't get this one…First of all, the most important thing is, you don't have to guarantee what you do. In other words, I can't guarantee that a Call Girl is going to give you the best whatever that you've ever had…I mean, of course, I can't *guarantee* that!

But, what I *can* guarantee you is that, when she arrives on your doorstep, she will look exactly the way I told you she was going to look! That she was going to be there *on time*! That she would be there exactly when I told you she would be there! Because this something that no other Escort Service did!

Basically, most Escort Services are really into lying, and basically the 'let me see if I can just get your money.' You know, '*your* money in *my* pocket tonight!' Regardless of what it is I have to tell you in order to do that!

So, they would routinely lie to clients and say, "Oh, you're looking for someone who is blonde? I've got someone who is blonde"… "Oh, you're looking for someone who is tall and busty? I've got just the right girl for you!"… "Oh, you want her there in half an hour? Sure. She'll be there in half an hour."

Well, an hour and a half later, a petite, flat-chested, red head knocks on their door. And obviously the client is going to be hideously disappointed. Which is actually very unfair to *her*! Because she doesn't know she's supposed to be a tall, busty blonde. And she's an hour late!

Anyway, so he ends up keeping her. But, he never calls again. So, that's not what we want! We want *repeat* business! But anyway, I'm getting off track.

So, my guarantee…When you're looking for a guarantee, the most important thing you can do is find out what complaints people have about other businesses that do what you do!

For instance, the biggest complaints about lawyers are, they don't return phone calls. So, if you're a lawyer, you can't guarantee that you'll win a case for somebody.

But, what you <u>can</u> guarantee is, "When you call my office someone will return your call within 12 hours or 24 hours", or whatever you want. Now, notice I said, "someone." They're not saying *I* will return your call. 'Someone will return your call.' It could be a lower level person, but *someone will return your call.*

Another one is, "We have a 24-hour service line that you can call at any time! A *live* person will pick up the phone!" You know, "We guarantee that a live person will pick up the phone and will do their best to help you with your problem."

Oh, I've got a really good one!...

This is something local on one of the local TV stations here. There's a Carpet Cleaning Business that advertises, and one of their big things is, "We don't charge you to move the furniture."

Who knew that carpet cleaners charged you to move the furniture?

But, apparently they do! And apparently they will quote you a real low price. But, then when they're done, and you actually get the bill, all of a sudden here's a $100 charge for moving the furniture that you weren't expecting!

So, if you're going to get your carpet cleaned, and you saw 'We're going to guarantee you that we aren't going to charge you extra..."

They're *not* guaranteeing you that they're going to get that spot out of your carpet. What they *are* guaranteeing you is they're *not* going to charge you to move the furniture!

Well, who are *you* going to call? You're going to call the person you feel the safest with!

The business where you're going to know what the bill is when it is all over. Where what they quote you is really going to be what it is going to cost you!

Because, if they're making that guarantee clearly, you sort of make the assumption… *That means other people charge to move the furniture*, and you don't want to get involved with someone like that.

So, what I would suggest for all of your readers, is to find out the biggest complaint that people have about people in your business, or your industry, then, see if there's a way to guarantee that you won't do that!

RDY: The funny thing is…Just yesterday on the radio I heard a commercial for a local gas station that gave a guarantee on the commercial. It said, 'If you get gas at one of our pumps, and use your credit card, if you have to come in to get your receipt, not only will *we* pay for your gas… But, you will get a cup of coffee *on us*! And, we guarantee that we'll send somebody out to fix the receipt machine.' (Because that's obviously why you had to come in for your receipt.)

They didn't guarantee the 'lowest price'!

They didn't guarantee to 'save mileage on your car with the best gas on the planet' or anything! But, they entered the conversation that was already in my head! Because that's a pet peeve of mine! Having to go in and get my receipt. I hate that!

So, I just thought that was a cool guarantee for a gas station...

SBB: Yeah, absolutely.

RDY: Now, in listening to what you've been saying... With the guarantee, and the way people answer the phone, and doing something special for your customers...

I'm starting to see the way all of this plays out in my head.

And, both of us being fans of Dan Kennedy... He talks a lot about movies that play in the customer's mind.

Now, for those reading who aren't necessarily familiar with what a "Mental Movie" is, and why it's important, can you talk a little bit about that and how you create that?

SBB: Yes. The minute that you appear on a customer's 'radar screen', they start the process of forming what we call a 'movie in their mind', which is basically expectations of what doing business with you is going to be like...

They start thinking about what they hope, or expect, that interacting with you and your employees is going to be like.

They start thinking about 'what is it going to be like when I come into their business?' 'How much are they going to charge me?'

You know, sort of 'What is it going to be like to do business with them?'

And so, that's the 'movie in their mind'.

So, what you need to do, just like I did in my former business, for the movie in my customer's minds from the minute they saw my ad was… 'Wow! This is a very upscale!" You know, "A classy business!"

Now, if I had some gum chewing broad from Brooklyn answer the phone, that would immediately ruin the movie they had in their mind!

So, I realized what I had to do to continue that movie is, I had to have someone answer the phone who spoke really beautifully, and was very warm, and friendly.

Actually, I have out of work actresses. Because there's a ton of those in New York, Lord knows!

And then, every single step of the way, the way we spoke to them, the way we asked them questions, the way that we... for instance, we never said, "How would you like to pay for this tonight?"

We always said, "How would you like to take care of this?"

Hey, everyone knows this is a business transaction. But, they don't want that! They don't necessarily want their faces rubbed in it, and their nose rubbed in it. So, "How would you like to take care of this tonight?"

Just everything we did was like that. Then, when the young lady got there, she would come in and shake his hand.

She wouldn't walk in and say, "Hi, my name is Suzy. Give me the money!" which is what everybody else does.

In fact, we didn't even get the money until the end. But, that's another story…

So, every step of the way, every touch that a customer has with you, whether it's in person, on the phone, with your website, with people who come out to do whatever voodoo it is that you do, everything has to be congruent!

It all has to maintain and support the movie, the image, that you want people to have in their mind about you.

RDY: So, as you're talking, I'm thinking back. Earlier you said something that I wanted to ask you about…

You said something about a 'Fresh Eyes Analysis'. So, what is that? And, why would every business need to have one at least once a year?

SBB: Yes. That's going back to what I was talking about before…

A *'Fresh Eyes Analysis'* is when someone comes in with fresh eyes who doesn't know you. And they can see what a customer sees, either a brand new customer, or someone you just see periodically.

This is really, really important. Because, you can't fix it, if you don't know it's broke. And, a lot of people just get... I hate to use the word 'sloppy'. But, in a way, that's what it is.

For instance, let's say that you're an Estate Attorney, or you're a Financial Planner.

When people walk into your office they're considering trusting you with their money.

I mean, you're not just in the Financial Planning Business. You're in the 'Secure My Future So I Can Sleep Business'!

Because, I know when I get older, I'm not going to be eating out of garbage cans...

I have a Disabled Child. I need to know they're going to be taken care of after I'm gone. So, I need to set something up, so I'll have the peace of mind that my child will always be taken care of! That's the business these kind of people are really in.

So, it doesn't look good if you have people that are real casually-dressed and if your office is very generic looking. When you're someone who is taking care of other people's money...

First of all, you want to look like you're very successful. Like you do a lot of business. You're very successful. You make a lot of money and your office reflects that! Very, very, very, very important!

Anything that is really generic... the client won't be able to put their finger on it. But, they'll say to themselves, "Wait a second. There's some subliminal thing saying, *How good could these guys be? Look at their office!*"

Everyone who works for someone like that should be wearing a suit. I mean, you don't want the girl behind the desk in some real casual outfit. I mean, there's nothing wrong with that technically. Not *technically*. But, sort of 'morally'.

There's a movie in your mind where you want these people to seem extremely stable. And very soft, or 'conservative' is a good word for this…

So, that means everyone who works for you needs to look and act very conservative.

Chiropractors, for instance, are not real Doctors… But, one of the things Chiropractors are often advised to do is that they, and everyone in their office, should wear one of those white lab coats.

That's a subliminal thing, because everyone associates that with Doctors.

So, that would be a very good thing for Chiropractors to do, to subliminally influence people in that way. So, that's what a 'Fresh Eyes Analysis' will do.

You come in, and you take a look around, and you see how could I improve the 'Mental Movie' that people are getting when they come into this establishment, when they do business with these people?

And, not only that, but can I tell you something?

You should do it every six months! *'Oh, come on, Sydney. That is very self-serving of you!'*

I know it sounds that way. But, the thing is, people flip-flop. So, you need to do it at least once a year. I mean, that's just not negotiable!

Every six months is better. But, even if you only do it just once a year, it's better than not doing it at all!

RDY: Right. Because, people get comfortable.

SBB: Well, believe it. You know, you see someone every day for 10 years. Their face starts to sag. They have some wrinkles. They gain a little weigh and get out of shape. But, you don't really notice it all that much…

But, let's say you went to a reunion, and you saw someone that you hadn't seen for 10 years. And all of the sudden they look like that. You would really notice it, because you hadn't seen them.

When you're very familiar with somebody, or something, and it slowly morphs in front of your eyes, you don't notice it the way you do when you see it, either for the first time, or for the first time in a number of years.

RDY: Yes. I teach a lot of Real Estate Investors and caution them that just because you get used to going out and talking with Motivated Sellers who are in a bad situation, that doesn't mean that you dress like them! You don't show up in jeans and a t-shirt, because that's what you were wearing sitting at your computer at your home office…

You need to actually dress up to go see them. Because, you'll get the 'Yeah, they're just like me' vote. So, you'll be more likely to get the contract signed!

SBB: Well, on the other hand, what you also don't want to do is, you don't want to show up in a really slick Georgio Armani suit. Because then, people are going to say to themselves, 'Oh, boy. This lady is really going to overcharge me!'

You want to show up in a nice pair of khakis. Maybe a nice woven shirt. You know, a nice pair of shoes. But, you don't want to over-do it. Because that sends the wrong message also.

RDY: Oh, yes. Now, you and Dan both believe that our economy is evolving into what I think you called an 'Experienced Economy'. What in the world is that?

SBB: Well, an *Experience* actually adds value to whatever it is you do or sell! Let's say there are a lot of people who do what you do...

How is someone going to choose? Why would someone choose to do business with you, over all those other people?

Well, unless it is a geography issue. Like, with Starbucks, it's whatever Starbucks is closer to you. Same with McDonalds. But, let's go back to your Real Estate people...

Why would someone choose to do business with you over all the other people that do what you do? Well, it's the Experience that they have when they do business with you. And experiences are really all about feelings.

In my book *Uncensored Sales Strategies* I actually have a list of 'Categories of Experiences'. Let me just pick a few...

 'What would delight them?'
 'What would be fun for them?'
 'What would make them feel unique and special?'

That is very important!

'What would make them feel good about themselves?'
'What could you do to make them feel safe and secure, give them peace of mind?'

That kind of thing!

So, for instance, Disney creates an incredible Experience! They create a memory Experience. They create something I could do with my family that they will love. Where I know I won't encounter anything I don't want my young children to see.

You know when you go to Disney, you're going to have practically a perfect outing, and Experience, and therefore memories of something that you did together.

So, creating an 'Experience' is very, very important!

For instance, with 7-11 stores... The Experience that a 7-11 wants to have is getting you in and out of there as quickly as possible.

But, if you're buying a Luxury item, the Experience you want to have is someone being attentive to you. Someone really listening to what you have to say, that sort of thing.

Also, visual is very, very big!

It's really important that when people walk in, that what they see delights them. That it pleases them when they look at it…

Another thing is, there's just incredible **homogeneity** going on in our society today. You know, you could be dropped into any mall in America. But, you wouldn't know where the hell you were. Because all of the stores are the same.

Everything is the same! You can go into any downtown area of any city and you're going to find a couple of banks, a couple of Starbucks. You know, no matter where you go everything is the same.

Well, if you stand out as someone who's different people are going to flock to you! There are reasons that some of these little coffee houses do better than Starbucks! It's because people want to go somewhere that's more unique. It has a little character. They feel like it's *their* special place!

They're not the kind of person that wants to go somewhere generic like Starbucks. They're someone who wants to go somewhere that's really unique!

Now, people who are accustomed to going to Dunkin Donuts, or McDonalds, for their coffee. To them, Starbucks *is* a unique Experience!

So, I'm not putting down Starbucks, I'm just saying that depending on who your customer is, you want to give them somewhere to go, and an Experience with you, that makes them feel that they're unique and special!

That you're unique, and special, and you're a real 'Find'. Also a really good Experience!

As a matter of fact, I was on a call with a bunch of dentists not too long ago and one of them asked me, "What can I do to create a positive Experience in my business?

Well, let's face it... No one likes going to the dentist! Nobody thinks it's a positive experience when they're going to the dentist...

So, one of the things I thought of… (And I actually got this from a Gynecologist's Office. Because, I had been in one that did this) is that when you're laying in that chair, and you're looking up at the ceiling, what do you see?

You see some kind of generic, yucky-looking ceiling. Well, what if you saw clouds painted on the ceiling? What if you were a child, and on the ceiling, there were all kinds of bright colored balloons, and animals, and all kinds of fun things to look at?

So, something on the ceiling that's different and unusual…

Do you know what's going to happen? Not only are they going to have a better feeling about being there. (I mean, nobody likes having their tooth drilled.)

But, at least being able to look at something that's attractive looking while you're having your tooth drilled, makes it a little bit better!

But, what it really does is, when you leave there, you're going to say, "Oh my! I just went to this dentist, and you wouldn't believe!... That dude had balloons, and animals, and all this bright stuff on the ceiling! I mean, I just couldn't believe it. It was really fun!"

They're going to tell that story to several different people! Now, if someone comes to them and says, "I'm looking for a dentist..." They'll say, "Oh my! You have *GOT* to go to *my* dentist! I have *such* a great dentist! You wouldn't believe what this guy has on his ceiling! It's just so much fun. It's fabulous!"

So, creating an Experience not only makes the person who is experiencing it happy. But, it gets word-of-mouth going around. Because they like talking about it! They like telling their friends about it!

So, if you can get an Experience like that, where people spread the word about you, because they were excited, and had fun, and a good time, and enjoyed doing business with you!...Then, what kind of better referral is there, than a really happy client, or customer, or patient?

RDY: I know exactly what you mean! My kids used to have a dentist where all of his chairs were in an open room. He had a drop ceiling. He took out all of the tiles in the drop ceiling, took them to a local middle school class, and they all drew art work on it!

So, he would talk to my kid in the chair, and say, "Hey, do you see that one up there with the giraffe? Isn't that a funny looking giraffe?" Or, "Hey, do you see the..."

So, they're looking as if they're having a fun conversation, and they don't even notice what's going on in their mouth. So, they enjoyed it! And I definitely enjoyed it! Because they came out smiling! So, that makes complete and total sense!

Now, we've all heard the old saying; *'It's not what you say, It's how you say it.'* But, as usual, you go even further... You talk about how certain words are more effective than others, and that they can create an effect on others, too.

I mean, I completely agree as a copyrighter. You know, I get paid for the way I arrange words on paper. But, can you give us some examples of what you mean by that?

SBB: Well, for instance, the word 'Appointment'. You know, there's nothing really wrong with the word

'Appointment'. But, 'meeting' or 'visit', if it's appropriate to what it is you do, would really be a better choice of words.

Most people when they hear the word 'Contract' think "Oh my! Lawyers, Problems, Money…" So, you'd be much better off calling it an "Agreement", or "Paperwork".

You're better off calling your people "Clients" or "The people we serve", instead of "Customers"!

You don't want to use words like "Cheaper" either. Better options are things like, "More economical" or "More affordable". Then the *way* you say something creates an effect too.

For instance, in my former business, I remember starting out answering the phones, you know? And, when I would say to a client, you know, by the time we figured out who he wanted to see, where he was, all that kind of thing, and the time she would be there, it got to the point where I would have to ask them their name…

Because, I'm not going to send a young lady over unless I really know who he is. But, I realized that when I asked them, "What is your name?" Oh my! I could feel their throats close! I could feel their stomachs contract right over the telephone line!

And, we would lose people a lot of times doing it that way. Because, it's like, "Oh my! They want my name. I don't know who's on the other end of the phone. How do I know they're not tape recording it?"

I mean all these fearful thoughts go through their mind! So, I started asking, "What name are you registered under? Or what name is your phone listed under?" Now, that's the same question. But, when you ask it that way, it's a lot less threatening!

Another example is that I used to say, "How would you like to take care of this?" Instead of, "How are you going to pay for this tonight?" There's a big difference with that, too!

I remember I had a client who had me come and consult with him. He had a trade show. And he was selling like a big package of stuff.

Then, when you bought the big package of stuff, you were automatically enrolled in a program where every month you would receive more stuff, and you got charged on your credit card every month. So, people would come in, and there's this long form to fill out. Name, address, phone number, blah, blah…

Well, a lot of people would say, "Gee, can't I just give you my business card, and you can staple it to the thing, so I don't have to fill all this out?" Well, the answer was usually yes. But, then what the salesman at the booth was saying was, "But, you still have to give me your credit card number."

Well, do you know how many people we lost, especially with the whole identity theft and things that are going on today? Because, people just heard, "I want your credit card number." So, it would scare them. It's like, "Well, I don't know who these people are. These people could be anybody… How do I know what they're going to do with my credit card number?" So, a lot of people walked away.

Well, I was sitting there, watching this, and I was having Deja Vu all over again. Because it's the same problem that

I had with the whole name thing. So, I thought to myself, 'Ok, how can I fix this?' So, I tried it out myself a few times just to make sure that it worked.

And, what I would do is, I said, "Rather than have you fill this whole thing out, and write all this stuff down again… Why don't you just give me your Business Card, and I'd be happy to staple it, and save you the trouble?"

And, they would say, "Oh, that's great! Here's the card." Then, I'd say, "Ok, there's one thing I need… I need you to personally fill it in from here down." And I would point to where the Credit Card information was.

And, do you know what? I didn't lose a single person! Because, I didn't say, "Give me your Credit Card number." I said, "I just need you to fill it in from here down." So, that just sounded less threatening. So, I told this to all the other guys. And they started doing it too. Well, I have to tell you, the *Walk-Aways* decreased down to almost nothing! It made a huge difference!

So, how you say something really *is* key, and it really *is* big!

The thing is, a lot of people have to understand this, and a lot of people don't want to hear this, but you actually have to do some of the selling and interacting with the customers yourself in order to realize, understand, and figure out what some of these problem words, phrases, or questions might be! It's easy to sit down, and write a script. You know, it looks real good on paper. But, you don't necessarily know how it's going to play out when the people who work for you actually use it and say it to people.

So, I would strongly suggest that everyone reading this, if they have people doing any kind of customer interaction for them, do it themselves and hear the kind of questions that people ask. Do it enough so you can feel the hesitation when they're asked certain kinds of questions. Because then, and only then, can you do something about it!

RDY: Now, I have told you repeatedly how much I'm absolutely in love with your book! The thing that stuck out to me was in Chapter 11, where you talked about 'Sales Choreography'. Because that wasn't a term that I had ever heard before. But, now I know what it's all about. So, I would love for our readers to hear it. Because it's just so powerful!

SBB: Ok. Well, 'Sales Choreography'...First of all, I would like to say that it could be either physical or psychological. A lot of times it's both! But, it's real purpose is to influence the perception that a customer, client, or patient has as a view of your business.

You want to influence them to make a purchase, or you want to control or influence the way a customer responds to you and your staff. You want to control, or influence, the way they move around in your space.

You want to control the way they think of you. You want to influence their perception of you who are. So, if you charge a high price, they're already expecting it. So, it's not out of the blue. So, it's not incongruent with every *Mental Movie* that they've developed of you so far.

It's very, very important! And let me just give you a couple of ideas...First of all, let's take a product.

You know, a woman goes into a store and she sees a mannequin with a skirt, a blouse, a belt, jewelry, a bag, and shoes. And a lot of times they will say to the sales person, "I want it to look exactly like that."

Now, if they had wandered around themselves to pick out all the different little pieces… First of all, they probably wouldn't do it, and second of all you could sell more when you put it all together for people.

Let's say you are in the Ipod selling business. If you put the Ipods on a table, and you have special little earbuds with jewels on it… (But, not the earbuds that come with it, because everybody gets that. But, let's say you have little earbuds with jewels on it, and you have a cute little carrying case.) And you have all these little Ipod things on a table…Well, a lot of times, people will just buy the Ipod. But, you might also sell all the other stuff that goes with it, too, or at least some of it. Now, if they had to wander all over the store, and try to pick out this stuff on their own, they probably wouldn't do it.

Now, Disney does *incredible* choreography! After you leave a certain ride, right after the exit for that ride, is a store, or a stand, or whatever, that has stuff for sale that is all the stuff you would think of, or that you saw during your experience when you went on that ride. And that is *'Sales Choreography'*. They have it right there!

So, you're under the influence of it. Your kids are under the influence of it. And they have a much better chance of selling you something if you see it right after you have been on the ride!

Why do you think things like candy, and gum, and little pick up items like that, are always near the register in stores? It's because it's an impulse purchase. *That* is 'Sales Choreography'!

Here's another Sales Choreography example I did. Let's take 'Psychological Choreography'... Beauty is very, very subjective, and no matter how accurately I might describe a young lady. There's no way that she's going to look like the movie in a guy's mind.

So, imagine a guy was to open the door, and a girl was standing very close to the door...

The first thing he'd see is her face. So, there would probably be a bit of a wave of disappointment. Because, it's very unlikely her face is going to be the face that he imagined or would be attracted to.

However, what I told my young ladies to do is, after they knocked on the door, to step back a few feet. So, when he opened the door, his first view was of all of her. You know, the shape of her body, the way she was dressed....

I used to call it the 'Totality of Her Presence'. In other words, after he got the whole picture in his mind first, which was always positive, then he would finally get to focus on her face. So, he had already had positive feelings in his mind. So, it was much more likely that he would find her face attractive. It was very important to me that the clients treat the young ladies politely and respectfully.

In fact, one of the reasons we always called them "young ladies", was because we wanted the clients to know that we considered them young *ladies*. And that we expected them to consider them young ladies, and go, and treat them like that. So, when the young lady would get there, first of all, they always wore suits, or a dress. And they very often would have a coat.

So, when they would walk in, and they went to take off their coat, or their suit jacket, what I told them to do was to stand in front of the male client. Turn maybe three quarters of the way around. And start to slide their coat, or their jacket, off their shoulders, which caused the man to instinctively reach, and help her with it. Just like any gentleman would do...

It's very, very subtle. But, it made the men think, 'I'm treating her like a lady' kind of thing. So, that's Physical and Psychological Choreography going on at the same time. Does that make sense?

RDY: Oh, it makes complete and total sense! Ok. So, I'm just going through the little Check List in my head...You've got the *Uncensored Sales Strategies* book. You've got a busy Consulting Practice...

It seems like you're out there on every stage in the nation. Because, you speak publically so often! What else are you up to? And what are you working on? What's coming down the pipeline for you next?

SBB: Well, experience is so important because you need to stand out from your competition!

You want people: A to spend their money with you, and B you want them to spend maybe more money than they were planning on spending. The #1 way to do this is to give them a positive experience when they do that.

Now, there are a lot of smaller businesses that simply can't afford the $5,000 a day, plus expenses, that I charge for my private consulting clients. So, what I did is, I created a six-month program where people get to spend a lot of 1-on-1 time with me every week. They spend 1-on-1 time with me on the phone. Then one week each month there's a group call. The group is small. The groups are only eight people a piece. This way we can discuss and customize what experiences would be good for your business.

Every other week there's a 15 minute 'Stay-On-Track' call where we talk about what you've done and how far you've gotten with things. And you can ask me questions. We can basically track your progress. The group call is a Mastermind Call. And, as you know Rachel, masterminding is just one of the most important things you can do!

Because everybody has a different perspective. Everyone has different experiences. Everyone has different resources. Everybody sees things differently than you do. And, if you try and run your business solely from your own point of view, you're really going to lose out. Because, not everybody you're trying to sell to thinks like you. So, a Mastermind is really a great idea!

Because it lets other people give you ideas, and suggestions, and strategies for, perhaps, producing an Experience that you want to produce for marketing. And for just all different kinds of things!

So, I'm doing that, and the sales page isn't up yet. But, my website is www.SydneyBarrows.com.

Then, I'm also working on an 'Experience Project' that people can buy, and they'll get all of the worksheets, and everything that I use with my private consulting clients. There will be CDs telling them how to use it. But, I'm trying to work with people to improve the Experience that customers and clients have when they do business with them.

RDY: Fantastic. So, for readers of this, you should know that if I trust her enough to have her in this book, then she is somebody that you're going to want to focus on, and stay in contact with! Sydney, thank you so much...

SBB: Oh, thanks for giving me this opportunity to share.

****Jason Oman's comment on Sydney Biddle-Barrow's chapter****

One of the great things Sydney talked about is to notice what other businesses are doing that is successful and see if there's a way that you can model it for your business.

The most important thing she said is that you should create a memorable experience for each and every customer. Make them feel unique and special by making their time with you an exceptionally pleasant experience.

In fact, creating awesome Experiences for people to enjoy and be WOW'd by is one of the smartest moves you can make!

Because, it not only keeps them coming back to your business, but it can also get them telling others & spreading the word for you!

Chapter 8:

Sandra Yancey, CEO and Founder of the eWomenNetwork

Rachel D. Young: With me today is Sandra Yancey. Sandra is the founder of the eWomenNetwork and is one of the best rags to riches stories that I've heard in a very, very long time!

I'm *so* excited to get to talk with you today. And, first of all, let me say thank you, Sandra, for making the time to be on the call. I know you're a busy lady.

Sandra Yancey: Well, I haven't met a woman yet that isn't crazy busy, right? So, everybody has their story.

RDY: Exactly. So, let me ask you this... Because you're a *very* successful business woman! You've got everything moving in just this incredibly positive direction! *eWomen Network* is growing so fast, but still at a very steady pace...Can you take us back to before *eWomen Network* ever came about? I mean, were you a corporate exec? Tell me about your life before entrepreneurship.

SY: Right. Well, I did 13 years in corporate America all with one company. I worked for a company called the *Mead Corporation*, which does school and office products.

It's a paper company. I spent half my time on the paper side of the company, and half my time on the paperless side of the company.

Ironically enough, they also owned Lexus Nexus which is online legal research, news research. I spent half of my time on the high tech side alone.

I had been marred 15 years and had a little girl. I just wanted to get into a situation where I could better manage my schedule. So, I quit and I went out on my own. I think I had my practice about seven years. Part of that was full-time. I launched it while I was working that last couple of years. And then, you know what? I realized, to be honest with you, that I had kind of reinvented my nightmare. I was a solo-preneur. So, I wasn't really behaving as a CEO, chief executive officer.

I was behaving more like a COE, the Chief of Everything. I was just doing it all!

I was doing my accounting and my Quick Books. I was doing the scheduling of things. I was doing all the follow-ups. I was doing all the paper generation materials, label mailing, everything, in advance, before my consulting assignments!

And I had a very sexy portfolio of clients! I mean, I had Coca Cola as a client. John Deere was a client. Levi Strauss was a client. APT was a client. Dow Jones. I just had this amazing client base and I was just absolutely living 24/7 on a plane! I was miserable!

I looked at my husband and just said, "You know, here we are. We live in Dallas, Texas, a major metropolitan city!"

And about 10 miles from my house at the time was this unbelievable complex of major corporations!

The world headquarters for Frito Lay was in Plano, Texas. The World headquarters for JC Penny's, and Ross Perot's EDS, and Cadbury Schwepps, the big huge Countrywide Insurance campus. Amazing corporations, of which none of them were my clients!

My husband said, "You know, they should be your clients! They would probably hire you in a nanosecond. They just don't know you exist!" So, I really started thinking about this whole notion of being a small business owner. We really *are* like these little soda cans floating out in the middle of the ocean!

I mean, we just don't have the marketing muscle to be able to brand ourselves in a way that people who need our products and services can really find us.
And, I thought, you know, it's really right!

So, I immediately started thinking about, 'Ok, I need to find out what's going on in Dallas. How do I get to meet people?'

Because. I met my other clients who were all from the Mead Corporation. Many of them had gotten laid off as Mead sold themselves and became second best.

So, those people ended up in these major corporations who remembered me. Do you see what I am saying?

I ran a P&L center. So, we charged back for our time so people knew that we had to do quality work. And that's how I picked up these clients. So, I thought, "Gosh, I've never really networked before as an entrepreneur." So, I decided, let me go networking.

So, back in 1999, I went to a networking event and it was the true, stereotypical description of the 'Good Old Boy's Club'! I marveled at it! You know, I wasn't angry at it. I didn't resent it. I mean, I just stepped back and said, "Look at what they got going on here." And, "this is impressive!"

I mean, how could this ever be criticized? It's so impressive, just the effectiveness in which I saw men show up for each other and men bringing their protégés.

The young, the bright, the bright-eyed, and showing them the ropes. And introducing them, helping them, and, you know, clearly men supporting men in business.

I just thought this is... no wonder men are in the position that they are! No wonder they so more readily build multi-million dollar businesses than women entrepreneurs! Only two percent of all women entrepreneurs ever generate a million-dollars in revenue. And yet we start businesses at the rate of two to one to men!

I'm thinking 1 out of every 11 adult women right now is an entrepreneur, owns her own business. And I'm thinking, gosh, I mean, no wonder! They are *so* supportive of each other, giving contacts, leads, information, resources, you know, business! So, I thought, 'hmm I have to do something here!'

Because, I didn't really feel like I had a chance to really be in the game. I felt like I was watching an amazing game! But, I was relegated to the stands. And, the best I could ever be was a fan… And I wanted to *play!* So, then someone said to me, "Well, you know, they have entrepreneurial women's groups."

I didn't even know that in 1999. So, I was like, "Really?"

So, I looked it up. I went to one. And, at the time, back in 1999, the particular event I went to, I felt like it was just really a *Social Experience!*

I felt like women did everything in pairs! They showed up with their girlfriend. They mixed and mingled with their girlfriend. They sat with their girlfriend. They watched the speaker with their girlfriend. They left with their girlfriend. You know what I mean?

And, I'm thinking, *No wonder women keep saying, "Well, I'm not growing my business,"* you know? I felt like if I interrupted, and I asked about their business, I felt like people looked at me as if I was intruding and going into an area that was not welcome.

So, I came back. I told my husband. We were talking about it and I just thought, *there has got to be other women, like me, who are clear about their competencies, and have a passion to run their own business, want to monetize it, and want to make serious money!And I just don't see a format that really allows women to do that!*

So, that's when I really started thinking about putting together my own Networking Group that would be really focused on networking in the way that women network!

Because women experience *so much* around the world differently than men! It's not right to wrong, better or worse. It's simply different!

And I believe Networking is really giving and not getting. Networking isn't about *'What's in it for me?'*, *'What am I going to get?'*, or *'She who collects the most cards wins!'* Or, some crazy thing like that. I believe Networking is more about building great relationships, which is something that you can do in a very speedy way! It's really about slowing down. It isn't about quantity at all. It's about having a very <u>core</u> set of *real* relationships and constantly looking at expanding that!

But, it isn't what Rolodex Builders do, you know? It isn't about building a database. It's building great relationships! So, it takes a little bit more time. It's a little bit more of a slower process. But, way, way, way, *way* more effective in the long run!

And then I thought eWomenNetwork needs a process that's unique to allowing every woman to have her voice, say who she is, what she does, and how she differentiates herself from other people that do what she does, and to ask exactly for what it is that we need.

Because we don't do that well, not in our personal lives, let alone our business lives! And that began the whole concept of *eWomenNetwork*.

RDY: Well, now, let me ask you this…Because, I know hindsight is always 20/20…I mean, it sounds like it was this sequence of events that were just common sense, from realizing that you had created a job that you owned, to understanding that you need the network and understanding that women that work different... it seems like it's all common sense now. At the time, did you ever feel lost, or were you always able to...

SY: Oh, oh, no. Never in a million years could you have told me that I was going to give up my consulting practice to build a Networking Company! You know, I was trying to satisfy a need I had, that I could not find in the marketplace. And then it dawned on me. Wow. You know, maybe I'm not alone!

So, I started asking my friends. I started calling my colleagues from Graduate school, the women, and asking them what they were doing, and what challenges they were having. And, as we began to talk about it, I thought, "Oh, this is more than just ballast. This is clearly a national, if not international opportunity here! But, where I made my mistake was that, at the time, if you remember, 2000, the internet was still relatively new…

And everybody was talking about the Internet in 1998 and 99. It was the big boom. The big explosion of Internet Businesses.

So, "eWomenNetwork" and the reason why it was originally E, was for electronic. It was the original kind of FaceBook, if you will, for Business Women!

But, the problem was it was an idea before its time. I mean, everybody was still on dial up back in 2000. Most people were on 'plain text'. There was no color, and richness, and photos, and video, and everything that it is today!

So, what I wanted to do, when I did my original focus groups, and I was writing the business plan in the focus groups, the women said to me, "I can't attend another meeting." I was like, "My, I can't get done what I have on my plate NOW, for crying out loud!" I mean, the last thing I can do is add one more thing!

And I listened to that. And I believed it! I believed that women have a lot of 'Shoulds' in their head that guides them to think a certain way.

But, the truth of the matter is, we make decisions in terms of business with people we trust, or through the recommendation of someone we trust overwhelmingly.

And, I thought it would be a FaceBook. And I went broke. I mean, I was on the brink of... of Bankruptcy! Two years into it I thought I'm losing everything I own. Because, I kept throwing money at it, and just working harder, and harder, and harder!

Well, I learned a valuable lesson. Sometimes you *do* have to listen to what they say! But, sometimes you have got to be open enough to step back and observe. Sometimes, I think, you have to watch the way your customers buy, and not just listen to what they say!

Then find that space that overlaps. Because, I was getting some members, but nothing to pay a bill. You know, I was robbing Peter to mug Paul. Do you know what I mean? Calling the light company and saying, "What is the least I have to pay to keep the lights on, so I can go pay the phone bill?" You know? And so, it certainly wasn't happening fast enough!

Then, when women were becoming members, they weren't posting their Profiles. They weren't taking the time out to post, because the whole search engine concept was very new in the beginning. Remember? People weren't utilizing Google to go do massive searches. It was still very fresh and new for most people, that concept. So, while some people said, "Hey, this sounds great," others really weren't doing it.

And then, one day, I got a phone call from a woman who said, "Hey, listen. I have been a member for about five months. I just put my profile up and I'm wondering if you have other members that live in my area that don't have their profile up, too? And maybe I could give you some of my surroundings cities. And, if you've got people, would you give me their names, their contact information?" And, I said, "Well, what would you do with that if I did that?"

She said, "Well, I would invite them for coffee, and we would get together to talk about our businesses."

I thought, "Oh, that's what you just said you didn't want to do," to myself. You know, in my focus groups you said you didn't have time for this. You didn't want to do it. That was when I got the real 'Aha' moment…

And it was a very powerful lesson for me that I utilize to this day! One of the most powerful things I do is to listen to the way my customers buy! So, even today in eWomenNetwork, we do surveys all the time. And, we garner data on a scale of 1 to 5.

What's your biggest challenges?
If you could wave a magic wand in your business...
How do you feel about the economy?

You know, we do all kinds of surveys, and we're always gathering information.

I still do at least a 40 city tour, this year almost 50 city tours, and just get out there. Because, I've learned so valuably that just having that hard data isn't everything. And you can make some real critical decisions that can really hurt you and lead you astray. You have to also be observant. You have to be in the field. You have to interact with your customers. You have to not only listen to what they say, but watch what they do.

And that's when, for me, the miracle started to begin! And we shifted. We not only have what is now a phenomenal photographic database of women professionals and entrepreneurs. But, we also have the Events. We don't call them 'meetings'. We call them Events. Because of the powerful differentiation of what each one of those words represents in our minds…

An Event is much more exciting! But, we have Events now. We do over 2000 events a year in this company to help women! And I think, Social Media is discovering that!

I mean we're hearing increasingly about the unfortunate predators. And I don't mean just sexual predators. But, predators that will take advantage of you. That you can't trust.

People, who aren't who they say they are on the internet. And that's why even Social Media Groups are now creating Meetups, right? Because, particularly as it relates to women, there's ultimately nothing that's more impactful than eye to eye, face to face, belly to belly interaction.

RDY: Well, now let me ask you this…Because, when I first got started in business, I started in Real Estate, and then moved to teaching Real Estate Marketing.

And, at one point, at the height of the Sub-Prime Craze when everybody was out buying Real Estate, I said, "You know, this is not going to last forever." And "I'm seeing some really dark clouds on the horizon."

So, I created a product about what is going to happen when this all falls. I even went to market with a book on the downfall of the Sub-Prime Market.

And I felt kind of like Noah, you know, that...

SY: Right, right, right.

RDY: "Hey guys, The end is coming. And it is going to be 'XYZ'." And everybody was just like, "No, no, we're pretty good making hand over fist. How can this not last forever?" And, as a result, I put so much into trying to warn people, and teach them with my products and my services. And because they didn't take off, I wound up doing the exact same thing...

I went completely belly up. It was so depressing and so frustrating. And, I know what it took for me. But, let me ask for you...

When you were trying to do this strictly online, and it just wasn't working, and you were facing bankruptcy, and I totally know about trying to put off the phone company, so you can pay the electric bill, and everything else...

What kept you from just going back and getting another job?

SY: I called my mother... true story. I called my mom. I was really clear that, you know, I had two children. I have a 19 year old daughter and a 14 year old son. So, 10 years ago they were 9 and 4.

I had one that wasn't in kindergarten yet. And, I had gone through all my funds, you know, and all my credit cards were maxed out. And I was like... "Ok, I cannot pay this bill. So, I can make the mortgage… And then, next month, I won't pay that bill. But, I will pay the other bill I didn't pay, so that I can... "

You know, just barely keeping things afloat. And I was like... I have *got* to go get a job! And, I called my mother. And we were just talking…

I didn't call her to tell her I was getting a job. I was just calling her to touch base with her. She was asking me how I was doing. And, of course, I started crying and I just was like... "I just can't believe that I can't fix this. I am not a stupid woman! I mean, I'm not the sharpest tool in the tool shed, but I'm not the dullest one either! I mean, I'm an educated woman. I have got a good almost 20 years in experience of a great job making a great salary. I had a great practice. And, of course, I was doing some little things on the side, you know."

And, my mother just basically said to me, "You've got one foot in your consulting practice, and one foot in this, and… are you becoming kind of good at many things, but a master of nothing?" And then I thought about that thing… You know, you can never steal 2nd base and keep your foot on 1st. And, I think there's a space where sometimes we are straddling two things.

And I had to ask myself, A: was I really 'Giving it everything'? The answer was "No".

And then, B, I said, "Well, I'm so far in debt now, the only thing that I can do that will bring me a sense of calm is some kind of stable, regular income. To get a job."

My mom said to me one question. My mom is an educated woman who's not even from this country, and she said to me, "So, let me just ask you…" She said, "How do you know it is high time to quit? I mean, how do you know that you're not effectively quitting five minutes before the miracle begins?"

And I went, "Wow. You know, I don't know."

She said, "Well, then you can't quit. It's not that you shouldn't quit. But, it's just that when you do quit, you need to be *really* clear that it's completely and totally the *right* thing to do!

Otherwise you will quit and you'll have regrets and you'll always wonder…"

I said, "Well, then what do I do?"

She said, "Well, I don't know, honey. I mean, I can't tell you what to do. But, I can tell you that I raised a daughter smart enough to figure it out."

I just remember going, "Wow!" And what I realized, Rachel, was that there's that old thing that's called 'Fake it till you make it.'

And, I don't subscribe to that. I actually don't believe in that. And my belief is actually that, that whole philosophy is what's behind why so many women struggle in business! And it's that whole thing of saying, "Fine. I'm fine," when I don't mean it.

RDY: I totally understand!

SY: And, if you listen…. Men don't use the word "fine." I mean, you'll rarely ever hear a man say the word "fine."

And women only say fine when they don't mean it, or when they don't care.

Like when you meet somebody at the elevator…

"How are you doing?"
"Fine. How are you?"

You know, you don't even mean it. It's rhetorical.

Or, when the people that love us the most that we're frustrated with, and we're huffing and puffing, they say, "You know, how are you doing? Is something wrong?"

"No, I am fine." And that's that whole 'Fake it till you make it' kind of concept that bleeds over in business.

The truth of the matter was when everybody was saying, "How's it going, Sandra?" I was like, "Oh, it's fine." I was embarrassed. I didn't want people to know. And I wasn't saying what I needed. And I just realized it was a real 'Aha moment' for me.

I was talking to a girlfriend about it who I really, really respect. We were just talking about her business and my business, and she is way, way more successful than me! To this day, *way* more successful, multi-*million* dollar woman business owner, the most wildly connected woman on the planet!

She and I were talking, and she said to me, "You know, Sandra, you have a lot of problems. And what you need is a coach!"

I said, "Well, I can't afford a coach. I'm broke."

She said, "Well, here's the one thing I know about women… And that is whenever we really want something, and we deem that it *is* of real value, we figure it out! Whether you pack up some of your kid's old clothes, and take it to a consignment shop. Or, you know, you get very resourceful! And, you're pretty resourceful, Sandra! You can figure this out!"

I was like, "Oh, my." So, I did. I went and got a coach… Then, I realized that I was so bogged down in the 'busy-ness' of the work, that I wasn't functioning on the business of the company. I wasn't focusing on the things that make the cash registers ring. I was being the 'technician', not the 'CEO'! I was doing it all! There just was *not* enough time in the day!

I needed to focus on the big vision of the company, and selling the company, and not doing... writing all of the script on the website. And, you know, directing all the new buttons, and this, and that, and the other. You know, doing *all* the invoicing, and the accounting, and the follow up, and the collections, and the... You know what I mean. I was doing it all! You name it. And people would join.

I was the person sending them the new Welcome Letter. You know, I was the person setting them up on auto billing. I was the person that was collecting when the, you know, credit card expiration date expired. I was the person, you know, I was... somebody told me, buy a bunch of t-shirts and sell them and it's free advertising. They will wear your logo.

And so I bought a bunch of T-shirts. And then I sold the t-shirts. And then it was me packaging the t-shirts and typing up the label. And it was me running up to the Post Office, and mailing them. And it was me... I mean, I was like doing it all! I was nuts. It was nuts. It was craziness as I look back.

And it wasn't until I stopped myself from saying I was "fine", and started being really honest, finding those people who I could be really honest around and admit to what wasn't working. Not to whine and complain. But, to say, "Here is my challenge. Do you have an idea? Do you have a contact? Do you have a lead? Do you have a resource? Do you have a good book? Do you know a great organization? Do you know…" whatever, fill in the blank. Once I did that, then I started to really see the miracle begin clearly.

Then, the next thing they said to me was, "Well, you've got to an employee. You're going crazy. There's only so many hours in the day. You've got 30 hours of work every day to get done. And there's only 24 hours and you've got to use some of them to sleep. So, you're just getting farther and farther behind".

And I just was like, "Oh, my... Now, what am I going to do?" Well, I have to go find an employee. So, I found an employee and I didn't want her to know, you know, 'I'm not even paying myself. How am I going to pay her?' Well, I found this woman, who is still with me to this day! She just said, "Sandra, I love what you're doing. This is amazing and I am your gal!

I can do all the infrastructure, the organizing. I can process the new members, and the Welcome Letter, and answer their questions about getting the profile up. I will be in the office doing all of that kind of stuff. You just focus on going out there and spreading the vision! And helping people see what it is you already see, and bringing them in to develop this community of great members!"

And I thought, "Oh, my..." So, I hired her and she said, "I just want you to know... I *do* have to be paid regularly! I mean, when you give me the check on Friday I need to be able to cash it!"

But, you know what? Do you know what happened, Rachel? Everything changed then for me. Because, on Wednesday, when I didn't have the money to pay her on Friday, you should have seen what I did!...

I just focused on selling, and making the cash register ring!

And then I had the money to pay her!

And then I started thinking… "My gosh, what is it about me that I don't feel myself worthy enough to put myself on the payroll, but *she* is worth it?

What's *that* about?" Then, that created a little bit of work, self-work that I needed to do. Then, I put *myself* on payroll and then everything started changing.

RDY: I'm just nodding so enthusiastically. I'm afraid my head may come right off my neck! You know, just to have all the things that you're talking about. Because, I think at one point, when I was at my lowest, I had to redefine for myself, the term, "Whatever it takes!"
That means, on my arms, I have scars from plasma donations I did three times a week for six months!

Because, that's what it took for me to be able to continue to pay the bills while I was trying to pick myself up from the doldrums of being depressed, or feeling like a failure. Like I had failed my family.

But, on another note, I will say that *you* have been one of the most professional people I've ever dealt with! And also your secretary, Leann, has been the easiest to work with!

SY: Really? She's amazing! I can't even imagine what I would do without Leann. You know, Leann, is my right arm! Anybody who ever wants to get to me has to go through Leann, as you well know. She's amazingly efficient!

She shares the same vision I have. We are *so* aligned in terms of being kind to people, being respectful to people, being nice to people.

And I've had employees that haven't done that. That I've had to fire. They come in and, you know, you're only as good as the people you surround yourself with.

But, when I originally hired Leann, she was a member. She had a franchise that wasn't going so well, and she needed some extra income. She had a background in Event Planning and I was starting my first conferences. So, I hired her Part-Time.

This was as a result of another member, Ruth. Leann and Ruth were friends. Ruth was a member of eWomenNetwork, and she was a financial advisor. But, she didn't ask me to invest with her, because I didn't have anything. I had a little bit of my 401K left at the time.

So, Ruth just really liked me. She saw me speak at an event. She just came up. She introduced herself to me. And she struck me as a very wise woman, a former executive with EDS. She had become a Financial Advisor with Ameriprise which, at the time, which was owned by American Express. And she said, "American Express needs to jump all over this! Let me see what I can do!" Within a week she had her local people in my office.

American Express did a local sponsorship. It was one of my very, very first sponsors. That gave me a tremendous amount of credibility and just opened the flood gates of other people paying attention to me! It's a high end, great reputation kind of thing! And people were like, "Ooh! Well, if American Express sees something in her and eWomenNetwork, maybe I should take a closer look." And then, boom, we got Microsoft and, boom, we got Office Depot.

Things started really turning around!

Ruth saw me going crazy still working way too many hours, and she said, "Sandra, you have got to get some help! I'm going to introduce you to someone. You can't afford *not* to utilize this woman!" And there was Leann…

Leann was a member of 'eWomen Network' and had her own franchise. She did custom dying of carpets. So, hotels used her if there was a stain. Builders used her if they had a home they wanted to change, because the new buyers wanted to change the color instead of replacing the carpet.

So, she had this franchise. But, it wasn't going as abundantly as she wanted it to go. And she wanted to pick up some stuff. So, Ruth introduced me to Leann. And I hired her on the spot.

And, of course, as the conference grew, we now do the largest 4-day Business Women's Conference in the nation! And, as the company grew, I offered Leann to head up the whole Conference Department and everything, or just be my 'right arm'. And this woman, you can't even imagine all the things she does for me! So, I have immense gratefulness for her! I can't even imagine being on the planet, and doing what I'm doing, without Leann!

RDY: Wow! So, on the paper you wrote the email address for me to organize this call, the ink on that paper got smudged, so I couldn't read it. So, I called and I thought, "Oh, gosh. How in the world am I going to find the Executive Assistant to organize this? You know, I'm just calling in out of the blue. Who am I? They don't know me from Adam!"

And I remember Mary Kay Ash always said, "Pretend that your customers are wearing a sign that says, 'Appreciate me.' Whether you know them or not."

And Leann was the very first of all of the Executive Assistants that I've dealt with where I felt like that sign was actually noticed. That she actually *did* appreciate me, and my time, and everything else.

I've had women scheduled to do an interview like this, and I've had their Executive Assistant call me and say, "Guess what? She's actually on a plane right now to leave the country unexpectedly and can't talk to you."

This happened 3 or 4 times before I finally said, "I would love to have you in the book. But, I can't have you doing this to my time." With Leann, I never felt anything less than appreciated!

So, I just wanted to let you know, that as far as Executive Assistants and the way that your business is run... It's obvious that not only is it successful, but you also have it very well-organized as well!

SY: Well, thank you! Thank you. Just so you know, I have my moments, OK? I've had those things where one of my employees changed an email that goes out, an automated email, and the wording that was received wasn't what her intention was. The impact of the wording was just strife with tremendous horror! I mean, people were mortified!

It was curt, and negative, and had a bad tone. I'm thinking, "Oh, my..." You know? And I had to jump in. The minute I heard it, I said, "Get me that email. I need to see it. We need to rephrase this, reposition it, rewrite it, and all that." But, there were some people that I lost. This is when members inactivated.

See, when you go inactive as an eWomenNetwork member, we have to very kindly and gently say, "You know, you can only come twice as a guest and then you need to join." So, if someone becomes inactive, we have to gently say, 'That means you can't come to the events.' Because we have Managing Directors who tell us, "Hey, this person went inactive. But, they keep coming to my events!"

But, there's a way to say that without saying, "You've lost all your privileges and that means that you can't do XYZ." There's a way to say 'We're going to miss you. And, we just want to remind you that when you leave, these are the things you won't have access to. We just want to make sure you're thinking that through. Because, we really exist to help you build your business.' Do you see the difference in the tone?

RDY: Oh, yeah.

SY: Same message. But, I just want you to know it hasn't all been perfect by any means.

RDY: No, but at the same time though, this was just *such* a pleasant experience from start to finish!...

Actually Linda Parrent and I were talking two weeks ago. And I actually joined eWomen Network at this last meeting.

SY: Oh, welcome!

RDY: Oh, thank you! A lot of that was just the overall experience that I've had with your company. Both, at an actual meeting, and dealing with Leann as well...

SY: Good. Well, good.

RDY: But, high praises to you for the way that your company is run! And, do you know what? That actually brings up a question...

Did you plan for *eWomen Network* to be this big? You know, when I read *Rich Dad, Poor Dad*, Robert Kiyosaki said, "Think and plan for the future and plan to be bigger than you are now!" And I just wondered looking at how big your empire has gotten… Did you ever imagine that it would be this big?

SY: Never! Never in a million years! Never in a million years… But, what I have learned is, and this is part of my big message on my tour, is getting women to really begin to embrace being incredibly successful!

You see, I think most women are a lot like I was. Which was probably more afraid of 'Will I have success?' than they were of even failing. Even now, in our conversation, I get nervous, and I have my own internal anxiety, when people say, "You've got an empire." And… "Now, that you're successful…"

I mean, look. I've got problems like everybody else. Can I just be honest? I'm reinventing like everybody else. There's a lot I *don't* know. And part of it is scary, sometimes, to not know. Because people think once you've got a staff, and you've generated multiple million dollars, that you now have it all figured out!

But, the economy has brought in all new barriers, and setbacks, and challenges, and opportunities. So, I've been navigating territory this last year that I haven't been in before. There is a lot I don't know that I'm still trying to figure out, you know? To maintain success, it's that whole thing.

The higher you climb, the farther you have to fall. So, to maintain a level of success requires constant new thinking. But, we have to adopt a philosophy, and an internal perspective of 'we can figure this out!' Not, "I" can figure it out, but "we" can figure it out! Most of the great ideas that come to 'eWomen Network' were seeds planted by somebody else that I just said, "Oh, I love that! What about *this* and what about *that*?"

We just spend time fertilizing it, and watering it, and nurturing it, and seeing it grow from this seed of a comment sometimes, to something that is a true transformational opportunity! Very few of those are my own ideas.

I think the *real* sign of a great leader is to be able to surround yourself with people that are *way* more talented than you! You know? *That* is when great success comes! When you have real fiscal responsibility.

Where do you spend money? You spend money on people that have ideas, and have competencies, and have experiences that *you* don't have! So, you can learn from them and leverage that which they can bring! Because, if I'm better than everybody else, or if I can do what everybody else can do... Then it's unnecessary. These people are unnecessary. I need people that can do and think what *I* can't do and think about! I mean that's really what they bring to the table.

So, it allows me to go out and do what I do best! Which is being really close to the customer, validating these ideas, listening to them, reassuring them, and giving them access.

I mean, that is what I see my job is… to give women entrepreneurs access to other amazing people. So, that they can get the right centering, the right contacts, leads, information, resources. To grow their businesses.

But, we have to think bigger! You know, we are thinking all day anyway. So, why not just think bigger than we normally think, and not get so caught up in, 'Oh, I don't know how to do that'? Well, you'll never know how to do *everything*!

I mean, who knows how to raise a child the first time? For that matter, who knows how to raise a child the second time? I mean, my son is so different from my daughter! It's like I'm raising two only children. But, you do it and we figure it out. We figure it out. And we don't do it *all* by ourselves!

We're talking to other moms, or finding other people to ask. You bump. You learn. You find out. They recommend this, or that person. That book. That organization that you need to be part of. Or, you know, stay away from that! Or, whatever…I mean, all of that! You're getting access from other parents on things that you're trying to do for your own children.

Well, business is the same way! But, the problem is, as women, we don't have access to other multi-million dollar women business owners, who are also happy, kind, and nice women.

But, I think we *can* do that! I don't think we have to give up that side of ourselves. We all know successful people who aren't happy! I'm looking for what I call *'Women that glow!'* Glow is that combustion of what happens when you're wildly successful and happy!

RDY: Exactly. So, let me ask you this…Because, you're talking about hiring someone, and making that realization that she is worth whatever it takes in order to pay her.

When I was working at the phone company, I would get up at four o'clock in the morning, leave my very small children and my ex-husband at home, and go to work. Then, come back after the sun had gone down, and they were all asleep.

But, when I went into business for myself, it was like, "Wow! *I'm* the boss! I don't feel like getting up until 10 AM." You know? All of the sudden *I* wasn't as deserving of getting up at four o'clock in the morning, or what have you... to work on my *own* business! To bring in those leads, etc.

SY: Well, we also don't have anybody keeping us accountable. And, let's be honest, you know? I mean, there's something about someone expecting you to deliver! And even *I* took that for granted!

Do you know what I mean? About just somebody making me accountable for delivering on certain things. And I wasn't doing that. You know?

So, I'm *really* clear that that's the power of getting a great coach! It's that it really *does* keep me accountable! Because, it's easy to kind of put it off. And say, "Oh, I will get to it tomorrow."

"Oh, I will start it on Monday… Why would I start a diet on a Thursday? Thursday is a silly day to start it. Because, Friday is the weekend. And I like to have my glass of wine on the weekend. And, by the way, we're going out for dinner on Saturday night. And I don't want to have to worry about… If I start on Thursday, then I'll feel guilty on Friday. Because, I'll know that I'm cheating. So, you know, let me just put it off. I'll just start on Monday!" That whole like 'crap' that we put ourselves through…

But, when you have somebody that's saying, "Look, here are your deliverables. This is when you have got to get this done, Ok? And, I'm holding you accountable. If the project is due on Monday, you work all weekend, and you re-arrange your schedules!

You maybe don't even go out on Saturday if you have got to have something delivered." Alright? It's kind of like studying in school. You have a test. If the students didn't have tests, they would never cram. They would never really study. There are these points along the way in which you have to deliver things. And for me that was a struggle, too!

You know, it was easy to say, "Oh, deal with this tomorrow." And, I also realized, as I looked back, that I wasn't making the cash register ring. Because, I wasn't working the phone. Because, the rejection was so great, and I was taking it so personally! So, I would go do 'Busy Stuff', because it made me feel competent. It made me feel like I could say I was working.

I look back at it. It just seems comical almost... this self-talk of how I hypnotized myself into thinking that I was really working hard. And that it was 'good enough'. And, the truth is, in business it's not about 'working hard'. Although you *do* have to work hard! So, let me just say it's not about not working hard. But, it *is* about realizing that it's about *results*, not activity! You *can't* do that! I get the numbers *every* day right now! Every day I'm working at the numbers. Every day! Three times a day. In the morning, I look at the numbers.

At the end of the day, I say, "How has the day gone?" Then I say, "Ok, which Managing Directors are showing a lot of results?" And I pick up the phone and make sure they are appreciated! "I saw what you've done. Congratulations, this and that..."

But, then more importantly, following up on the ones that are just at that *Tipping Point*. The problem is, we've put *so* much energy into the laggards, the people that are really struggling, and once you get them the fundamental training, if they aren't performing what we expected...

If you make a bell curve, right? On the right hand side, are the people that are your stars! They're just skating along. On the left hand side, before that, is the hump of the bell curve. Those are the people who are really struggling.

Then you have the top of the curve. And there are the people that are on the cusp of doing great.

We often ignore those people and focus on the laggards, the ones that are super struggling. What I've learned is that, in any organization you should strive for 20 percent stars. Do you know what I mean? And then 10 percent are laggards. Then, the rest of the 70 percent are just like the roller coaster, just above the top to going down. That's where you spend your time! What often happens is, we get usurped into focusing on all these people that are struggling, which were probably just really bad hires, you know?

RDY: Well, my husband said we need to do at least 3 things…We have our 3 things that we process every single morning before we even open emails. Before we update our FaceBook status, before anything else happens, these 3 things have to happen so that you know for the rest of the day, even if you get nothing else done, you will *still* have customers, and traffic to your website, and things happening that will continue to put money into the business.

And just being able to say, "You know what? I *have* to do these 3 things!" There's freedom in that!

Of saying, "I can't work on this right now! Because, it's *not* one of my three things!"

So, ok, looking back on everything that you've accomplished over the past 10 years, is there anything that you would do differently? I mean would you change any of it?

SY: Certainly! I mean, certainly I would do things differently! I mean, in the very beginning, my greatest obstacle was me!

So, I would have gotten a coach much sooner without question! I would've gotten a coach *much* sooner!

I would've gotten my first employee sooner. At least a year earlier! I would've perhaps even pursued *Venture Capital*! I didn't do that. I did it the hard way. I ended up giving up some small pieces, a very, very small percentage of the business. First, some partnerships to get technology support and graphic support.

My very first employee, I ended up giving her a very small percentage of the business. Because I didn't want to lose her. And she had everything rockin' & rollin' so wonderfully that I thought, "My, if I ever have to go back and do all this stuff I won't know how to do it anyway! I'll *never* figure out what she has done! And I don't *want* to do that! That wouldn't be a good use of my time anyway." And that proved to be really smart. So, if I could have hired her sooner, I would have done that sooner. Those were a couple of really smart moves that I made. I just wish I had done them sooner!

But, in order to do all of that, I would've had to have done better work on *me*! Around my own fears, and my playing it safe, and my not being authentic, and telling people 'Everything is great and wonderful!' when in reality I couldn't pay the bills.

Sure, if I had done it differently, I would've started events at the very beginning, versus spending two years trying to build just an online Search Engine Profile System! 2 years of, in many ways, of lost productivity. But, 2 years that have kept me very humble! And Rachel, I think it's really important that we never forget where we came from!

I think it helps me to identify with most of my customers, most of my members. Because I've been there! I understand it. I wasn't born with a *Silver Spoon*. I didn't have this instantaneous success! It gives me power. Because it makes me realize that I could lose it all…But, I have the strength and the ability to recover!

Failure doesn't define me. The lessons define me! So, if I don't learn any lessons, I'm in real trouble! And, you can make Fatal Mistakes. But, if you learned the lesson from that Fatal Mistake, you can rebuild. It's kind of like, when you're down and out, as long as you can look up, you can get up! You know?

RDY: My dad always says, *'when you get to the end of your rope… tie a knot, and hang on!'*

SY: Swing! My mom used to say *'swing! Tie a knot and swing!'* Because, if you just hang there, if you use that as a metaphor, eventually you'll lose the strength. But, if you swing, at least you have the chance of building momentum! And, when you let go, you might land, *not* in the pit. Do you know what I mean?

RDY: I love that! I love that! Just that one little tweak makes it. Oh, that's fantastic!

So, to the women who are reading this book and who may be afraid of taking that first step, or who are even afraid of failing at all, what do you say to them?

SY: Well, the first step I would say, is that you have to be clear of your commitment. We say 80 percent of businesses fail because of one thing. It's just your decision to be totally committed to your dream. I do this all the time with an audience…

I'll say to a sea of women. *"How many of you have wanted to lose 10 pounds?"* And, overwhelmingly 90 percent of the audience raises its hand…Then, I say, *"And that was last year. How many of you still want to lose the same 10 pounds?"* And the sea of hands, almost the exact same hands go up. Then, I say, *"So, I'm just curious to know... Do you not know what to do? How many of you don't know what to do to lose those 10 pounds?"* And no hands go up. *"How many of you know exactly what you need to do?"* And the hands go back up.

We know we need to eat healthier. We need to eat less junk and we need to move more. I mean, it's pretty fundamental. Now, I also say, *"How many of you feel like you need to spend a lot of money to do those things?"* Really? I mean, there *is* free access! On Google there's every diet recipe on the planet! Low Cal, Low-Fat recipe on the planet at your fingertips. You don't have to pay a nickel for it!

You *do* have the luxury to be able to use your legs and walk. You don't have to join a gym. Right? You can get a couple of big pork and bean cans for your weights, and you can get outside and walk. You can take an empty bottle, fill it with rocks, and lift, and that kind of thing. Do you know what I'm saying? I mean, you don't *have* to join a gym. You don't have to spend money. We all know what to do!

Why is it that some do it and some don't? Ultimately, it's just realizing, 'I'm going to decide, and make the commitment, that I'm going to get this weight off!'

And, once you've done that, no fabulous piece of Cheese Cake can tempt you otherwise! Nothing will get in your way. And you'll figure it out! So, you have to be totally committed to your dream! You have to know that you're entitled to your dream. That you were born to define your

Purpose. That Purpose becomes your dream and you're entitled to live your dream and shame on you if you don't! Because the world *wants* you to live your dream!

What you can contribute to the world, your 'legacy' is defined on your ability to embrace your passion and monetize it.

And, it gets bigger to say, "Do you know what? When I play small, that's not when I have real flexibility and control. And it's crap. That's crap!" When you've got flexibility and control is when you can build something. So, you really can go on vacation and the business keeps running!

If you go on vacation, and your business stops, you don't really have a business! That's a job! As Michael Gerber says, "You're working for a lunatic!" It's about building something bigger and not being afraid that you don't know.

But, you have to get comfortable with the discomfort of the not knowing. Because, no matter how successful you are, every level that you elevate to, you go back to zero. And you've got to figure it out again. But, the beauty of that is that you're always learning!

It's not just your business growing, but you're growing personally! Then simply never forget where you came from… When it's your turn to be in the Catbird Seat, don't fold your arms and say, "I did it. You figure it out!" We have to lift as we climb! We have to be there.

You have to help other people and not think, 'tit for tat' and 'quid pro quo' and 'you scratch my back and I'll scratch yours.' That's not what it's about! It's about… my mother used to say, "Give without remembering and take without forgetting." You know, give and don't remember!

Don't just know you're doing the right thing. Trust and it will come back to you 10 fold! If someone helps you, don't forget it! Don't forget to say 'Thank You'. Don't forget to brag about her.

I think when you do that, no matter what your obstacles are, you will overcome, or learn to become at peace. And ultimately you will have great relationships that will continue to give you access to rebuild. Who are we to play small? It's ridiculous! I mean, we're here. We're here for who knows how long? For many people, way too short! You've got to maximize it in every way we can!

And you will have your lonely, scared moments. That never goes away. But, it's what you do with those moments! Those moments are sometimes good to help you stop and reflect. They help you get in touch. They help you whisper words of praise in your own ear.

You don't have to worry about being unduly modest, if no one hears you boasting! Every now and then women are starved for appreciation. And sometimes we have to appreciate ourselves! We can't be the great mothers, and wives, and caregivers, and volunteers, and philanthropists in the world, if we don't take care of ourselves!

It's in taking care of ourselves that allows us to be able to do all these other great things! And taking care of ourselves is about taking care of ourselves physically and emotionally. But, it's also about making sure we make our dreams come true!

RDY: That's fantastic! I love everything that you just said! That's so beautiful. It gave me chills! I can't tell you how much I've enjoyed being able to talk with you today! Thank you so very much for talking to me today!

SY: You're so welcome! Thank you! I'm honored to have had this time with you, Rachel. Best of luck to you and keep me posted, ok?

RDY: Thank you. I certainly will.

Jason Oman's comment on Sandra Yancey's chapter**

If you need help, don't be afraid to ask for it. You don't have to figure things out all by yourself! There is plenty of help out there, in many forms. There's networking groups, mastermind groups, your friends, your business colleagues...they're everywhere!

To be a success, you have to work hard. But, the actions you take need to be actions that will create positive results!

Now, as you're preparing to launch yourself to the next level of success, it's likely you will have some doubt and some scary moments.

So, decide in advance that you will NOT let those moments hold you back! They can only affect you if you let them! You DO have the power to decide in advance not to let anything hold you back!

We believe in you and I KNOW you CAN do it!

Get More Information from Rachel D. Young!

Women account for over half of the businesses started in the United States today – but until March, 2010, NO WOMAN was teaching fellow entrepreneurial women how to RUN those businesses!

That is until Rachel D. Young founded Women Creating Wealth, an online training course featuring topics such as:

- **How to Write a Business Plan in 30 Minutes or Less!**
- Standard Operating Procedures: What they are and why you need them
- **Time Management for Busy Women**
- A Nerd-Free Lesson on How to Create a Website from Scratch for FREE!
- **How to Automate Your Marketing**
- The One Thing All Women Want but Don't Want to Talk About (hint: it involves money)
- **And much, much more!**

Join the community of female business owners (women-only, please) by visiting:

www.WomenCreatingWealthOnline.com

This isn't your average "Good Ol' Boys Club" and is NOT a networking group. You'll discover videos, audio interviews, and more with DETAILED INSTRUCTION on how to run a successful business!

In fact, we guarantee you'll walk away from each video with a set plan on how to implement exactly what you've just learned!

Get More Information from Jason Oman!

Now, Discover the Life-Changing Secrets Self-Made Millionaires Use To Generate Money Quickly & Easily Whenever They Want At:

www.MillionaireMoneyFormula.com/free

Learn From 9 More Amazing Self-Made Millionaires At:

www.ConversationsWithMillionaires.com

<u>Connect with Jason Oman in Social Media At:</u>

www.FaceBook.com/JasonOman
www.MySpace.com/JasonOman
www.Twitter.com/JasonOman
www.YouTube.com/JasonOman
www.LinkedIn.com/in/JasonOman

About Jason Oman

As a result of his success with his first business, Jason Oman was selected to become a 'Featured Success Story' on a highly-successful TV infomercial called *'Creating Wealth'* with 4 self-made millionaires.

Jason followed that up by creating his 'Conversations with Millionaires' book with 9 more self-made millionaires which became an instant #1 Best-Seller!

These experiences lead Jason to uncover the powerful steps highly-successful entrepreneurs use to generate money quickly & easily called the 'Millionaire Money Formula'.

Today Jason enjoys helping others change their lives by the secrets they dream of as well!

About Rachel D. Young

Starting her first business in the basement of a family friend's house, Rachel quickly raised herself from homeless, unemployed mother of 3 to become one of the nation's leading authorities on women-owned businesses.

Starting Women Creating Wealth, Rachel now teaches women of all experience-levels how to run a successful business, regardless of their niche or industry.

Rachel has also authored several groundbreaking books and CDs specifically for female entrepreneurs.

Rachel lives in Atlanta with her husband and 3 children.

www.ingramcontent.com/pod-product-compliance
Lightning Source LLC
LaVergne TN
LVHW051459080426

835509LV00017B/1822